Quickbooks

Learn Quickbooks Quickly and Improve Your Financial IQ. The Only Step-by-Step Guide for Accounting and Business

TABLE OF CONTENTS

By Carl Russell

Chapter One: Why, Quickbooks?

Let's begin with the essential question: Why do you need an accounting system like QuickBooks? It's a reasonable question, so let me supply the two-section answer.

The principal reason is that government law requires your business to keep up an accounting system. All the more explicitly, Section 446 (General Rule for Methods of Accounting) of Title 26 (Internal Revenue Code) of the United States Code necessitates that you have the capacity to register assessable pay by using a type of sound judgment accounting system that plainly reflects salary.

If you choose to brush off this prerequisite — all things considered, you got into business so you could lose the shackles of an organization — you may pull off your exclusion. In any case, if the Internal Revenue Service (IRS) looks at your arrival, and you disregarded Section 446, the IRS finds a good pace accounting for how it needs. And, the IRS way implies that you make good on additional in charges and that you likewise pay imposes sooner than you would have something else.

Here's the second purpose behind keeping up an accounting system. I kind of go out on an article appendage; however, I will do it in any case. My solid conviction — supported by over three many years of business experience and close-hand perceptions of a few hundred business customers — is that you can't effectively deal with your business without a not too bad accounting system.

Success requires precisely estimating success or losses and sensibly assessing your budgetary condition.

This subsequent explanation bodes well, isn't that so? If your companion Kenneth doesn't have the foggiest idea when he's creation cash, which items or administrations are productive, and which clients merit keeping (and which aren't), does he truly get an opportunity?

I don't figure he does.

To condense, your business must have a better than average accounting system, regardless of how you feel about accounting and paying little heed to how tedious and costly such a system is or becomes. The law expects you to have such an accounting system. Furthermore, fruitful business management relies upon such an accounting system.

What QuickBooks does

Go on to the following question that you and I have to examine: What does QuickBooks do to assist you with keeping up an accounting system that estimates benefits and misfortunes and other stuff that way?

QuickBooks really makes business accounting simple by giving windows that you use to record regular business transactions. QuickBooks has a window (you know, a Windows window that shows up on your screen) that resembles a check, for instance. To record a check you write, you fill in the spaces of the window with bits of data, for example, the date, sum, and individual or business you're paying.

QuickBooks additionally has a bunch of different windows that you use along these lines. It supplies a receipt window, for instance, that seems as though a receipt you may use to charge a client or customer. You fill in the receipt window's spaces by recording receipt data, for example, the name of the customer or client, receipt sum, and date by which you need to be paid.

Here's the flawless thing about these check and receipt windows: When you record business transactions by filling in the spaces indicated on-screen, you gather the data that QuickBooks needs to set up the reports that condense your success or losses and your financial circumstance.

Your accounting with QuickBooks can be similarly as basic as I describe in the past passages. As it were, if you record only a bunch of business transactions by using the right QuickBooks windows, Such reports can be used to figure benefits or (ugh) misfortunes for a week ago, a month ago, or a year ago. Such reports can likewise be used to compute benefits and misfortunes for specific clients and items.

I know I'm somewhat cruel in the initial segment of this section — raising that stuff about the IRS and business failure — yet this accounting stuff is flawless!

Great accounting gives you an approach to deal with your business for productivity. Furthermore, clearly, a wide range of good and magnificent things originate from working your business beneficially: a really agreeable life for you and your employees; monetary padding to get you through the extreme fixes; and benefits that can be reinvested in your business, in different organizations, and in-network noble cause.

Let me notice a couple other darn convenient things that QuickBooks (and other accounting systems, as well) accomplish for you, the exhausted entrepreneur or clerk:

Forms: QuickBooks creates, or prints, forms, for example, checks or invoices by using the data you enter in those check windows and receipt windows that I notice prior. With the goal that's slick, and genuine help.

Electronic banking and billing: QuickBooks transmits and recovers some budgetary transaction data electronically. It can email your invoices to clients and customers, for instance. (That can save you both time and cash.) And QuickBooks can share bank accounting data with most significant banks, making it simple to make payments and move reserves electronically.

Why not QuickBooks on the web?

Presently for an ungainly question: Should you use the work area variant of QuickBooks, or do you have to show some signs of life and use the online adaptation of QuickBooks? Great question.

My proposal is that you work with the work area adaptation of QuickBooks — the subject of this book. I base this proposal on two components:

The work area rendition is presumably essentially increasingly conservative throughout the years you use QuickBooks. The issue with these membership type estimating models is that you pay — after some time — way, route more for a thing. And, I accept this is valid with QuickBooks.

At any rate, right now, the work area rendition of QuickBooks gives greater usefulness and a more extravagant list of capabilities. I'm not going to list what is remembered for the work area form exclusively and missing in the online rendition; however, I see gaps. (I'm glad to stipulate that, truly, sooner or later Intuit will without a doubt plug these openings. In any case, meanwhile, hello, why pay more for less?)

Would I be able to call attention to one situation in which the online variant does bode well, notwithstanding its more noteworthy expense and lesser usefulness? If you have to have individuals in various areas (across town, the nation over, around the world, etc.) share QuickBooks, the online adaptation of QuickBooks rocks. It truly shakes.

Note: If your CPA can bolster your use of QuickBooks basically on the grounds that you're using the online variant, that may legitimize the additional expense and lighter list of capabilities.

What Explains QuickBooks' Popularity?

No question concerning it — you need a decent accounting system in case you're good to go. In any case, guess what? That reality doesn't clarify why

QuickBooks is so famous or why you should use QuickBooks. (I disregard for one minute the way that you've likely previously bought QuickBooks.) Therefore, let me recommend to you three reasons why QuickBooks is a great decision to use as the establishment of your accounting system:

Usability: QuickBooks generally has been the least demanding or one of the most effortless accounting programming projects to use. Why? The entire simply enter-transaction data into-windows-that-look forms thing (which I talk about prior) makes information passage a breeze. Most agents definitely realize how to fill in the spaces in these forms. That implies that the vast majority — most likely, including you — know nearly all that they have to know to gather the data that they have to do their books with QuickBooks. After some time, other programming programs have would, in general, become more QuickBooks-like at their convenience. The people at Intuit have genuinely made sense of how to make and continue accounting simple.

Cost: QuickBooks, particularly contrasted and the bad-to-the-bone accounting bundles that bookkeepers love, is pretty darn modest. Various adaptations have various costs; however, for a rough approximation, you can get an astounding accounting programming answer for two or three hundred bucks.

Not to go all grandfatherly on you or anything, yet when I was a youthful CPA, cheap accounting programming bundles frequently cost a few thousand dollars. And, it was practically simple to burn through a huge number of dollars.

Omnipresence: The universality issue identifies with the usability of QuickBooks and the modest value that Intuit charges for QuickBooks. Strangely, the universality of QuickBooks turns into its own advantage, as well. You'll see it exceptionally simple to discover an accountant who knows QuickBooks, for instance. Furthermore, if you can't, you can enlist somebody who doesn't know QuickBooks and afterward send that person to a QuickBooks class at the nearby junior college (since that class will be anything but difficult to discover). You'll likewise think that it's extremely simple to discover a CPA who knows QuickBooks. Presently, you may decide to use some other, excellent bit of accounting programming. Assuredly, in any case, what you'll find is that it's harder to discover individuals who know the product, harder to discover classes for the product, harder to discover CPAs who know the product, and significantly harder to discover books about the product.

What's Next, Dude?

Now, apparently, you know why you need accounting programming and why QuickBooks is presumably a sensible and possibly a magnificent decision. At the end of the day, you accepted my line about QuickBooks with barely a second thought. That choice on your part leaves the subject of what you ought to do straight away. Let me state this. More or less, before you can start working with QuickBooks, you have to do the accompanying:

1. Install QuickBooks programming.

2. Run through the QuickBooks Setup process.

3. Load the master documents

In case you're thinking, "Hold up, cowhand, that appears to be more work than what's associated with introducing coversheet programming or another word processor," you're correct. You should get notification from me the monstrous truth about accounting programming: Accounting programming, every last bit of it, requires a lot of alignment work to get things running easily. You have to manufacture a list of cost classes, or accounts, to use for the following costs, for instance. You likewise need to set up a list of the clients your receipt.

Have confidence, in any case, that none of the alignment work is excessively mind-boggling; it's simply tedious. Additionally, know from the very beginning that QuickBooks gives an enormous measure of hand-holding to assist you with venturing through the alignment procedure. Keep in mind that you have your new companion — that is me — to help you at whatever point the alignment procedure gets somewhat amazing.

The most effective method to Succeed with QuickBooks

Before I wrap up the little why, what, and how the discussion of this section, I should give a bunch of thoughts regarding how to make your involvement in QuickBooks a fruitful one.

Budget shrewdly

Here's my first proposal: Please plan on spending, at any rate, a couple of hours to get the QuickBooks programming introduced, set up, and running. I realize you would prefer truly not to do that. You have a business to run, a family to deal with, a canine to walk, etc.

In any case, here's the truth sandwich you most likely need to take a major nibble of It takes thirty minutes just to get the product introduced on your PC. (This establishment isn't entangled, obviously. You'll for the most part simply stay there, tasting espresso or whatever.)

In any case, after the QuickBooks programming is introduced, lamentably, you, despite everything, need to go through the QuickBooks Setup process. Once more, this work isn't troublesome; however, it takes time. Setting up QuickBooks for an extremely straightforward assistance business likely takes at any rate 60 minutes. If your business claims stock, or in case you're a temporary worker with some genuine job costing prerequisites, the procedure can take a few hours.

Hence, help yourself out: Give yourself a satisfactory time for the current task.

Try not to concentrate on highlights

Presently let me share another little tip about starting QuickBooks. At the point that you introduce the QuickBooks programming and start the program, you'll be in stun about the number of directions, whistles, chimes, and windows that the QuickBooks window gives. However, guess what? You can't concentrate on the QuickBooks highlights.

Your job is basically to make sense of how to record a bunch — most likely a little bunch — of transactions with QuickBooks. Accordingly, what you need to do is center around the transactions that should be recorded for you to keep your books.

Assume that you're a one-individual counseling business. All things considered, you may need to make sense of how to record just the accompanying three transactions:

Invoices

Payments from clients (since you invoiced them) Payments to merchants (since they sent you charges)

So you should simply find how to record invoices, record client payments, and record checks. You don't have to stress over much else aside from perhaps how to print reports; however, that is simple.

"Gracious, Becker," you're saying, "you just deliberately picked a simple business. I'm a retailer with a considerably more muddled circumstance."

Alright, well, you're correct that I picked a simple business for my first model; however, I remain by similar guidance for retailers. In case you're a retailer, you most likely need to make sense of how to record just four transactions:

Sales receipts

Bills from your providers' Payments to your seller's Employee finance checks

Right now, you should simply discover how to record sales receipts — presumably a different sales receipt for each bank store you make — how to record bills from sellers, how to record checks to cover your tabs, and how to deal with workers finance.

I would prefer not to be grouchy or reckless here; however, one genuinely great stunt for finding a good pace with QuickBooks is to concentrate on the transactions that you have to record. If you distinguish those transactions and then make sense of how to record them, you've done the critical step. Truly.

Payment to vendors

Here's another recommendation for you: Go ahead and redistribute your finance. That will most likely cost you somewhere in the range of $1,000 and $2,000 every year. I know that is generally the absolute expense of four markdown passes to Hawaii. However, re-appropriating finance conveys three major advantages, much in the wake of thinking about the firm cost:

Effortlessness: Payroll is one of the most convoluted territories in small business accounting and in QuickBooks. In like manner, you'll significantly streamline your accounting by moving this cerebral pain off your work area and onto the work area of your bookkeeper (the individual may cherish doing your finance) or the finance administration. (You can use a national firm, for example, ADP or Paychex, or a nearby firm.)

Penalties: Did I notice that finance would one say one is of the most confusing zones in small business accounting and in QuickBooks? I did. Great, since you genuinely need to realize that finance alignment and accounting botches are anything but difficult to make. And, finance botches regularly subject you to genuinely irritating fines and penalties from the IRS and from state income and work organizations. I award you that $1,500 every year for finance handling appears abundant excess cash, however, you have to forestall just two or three excruciating fines or penalties every year to radically reduce the expenses of using an outside finance administration.

Mrs. Peabody's yearly raise: One last purpose behind redistributing finance exists. Allow me to clarify. You would prefer not to do finance yourself. Truly, you don't. Therefore, you'll, in the long run, allocate the undertaking to that decent lady who works in your office, Mrs. Peabody. This is what will happen when you do that — late one evening time during the week following Mrs.

Peabody's first finance, she'll request to meet with you — to discuss why Mrs. Raleigh makes $15,000 more every year than she (Mrs. Peabody) does, and furthermore, to inquire as to why she (Mrs.

Peabody) makes just $2 every hour more than Wayne, the nitwit who works in the distribution center. Since you're a pleasant individual, Mrs. Peabody will leave a couple of moments later with a $1.50-per-hour raise. Furthermore, by then, you'll recollect, dubiously, my previous alert about the issue of sparing possibly $2,000 every year in finance administration expenses yet then giving Mrs. Peabody an extra $3,000 raise. Ouch.

Get proficient assistance

A fast point: You can likely get a CPA to plunk down with you for an hour or two and tell you the best way to enter a bunch of transactions in QuickBooks. At the end of the day, for a cost that is likely somewhere close to $200 and $300, you can have someone hold your hand for the initial three invoices you make, the initial two bills you record, the initial four checks you write, etc.

You should attempt to do this if you can. You'll save yourself untold long stretches of migraines by having somebody who realizes what she or he is doing give an itty-bit of customized preparation.

Use both the benefit and misfortune articulation and the balance sheet

Also, presently, my last point: You genuinely need to use your benefit and misfortune articulation (which gauges your benefits) and your accounting report (which accounts for your advantages, liabilities, and proprietor's value) as a major aspect of dealing with your business. As it were, become acclimated to delivering a QuickBooks benefit and misfortune explanation every week, or month, or whatever. Then use that announcement to decide your gainfulness. Along these lines, normally produce an accounting report to check your money balances, the sums clients or customers owe, etc.

Possibly this counsel appears glaringly evident, yet there's a semi-concealed purpose behind my proposal: If you or you and the clerk do the accounting accurately, both the QuickBooks benefit and misfortune articulation and the accounting report will show numbers that bode well. As it were, the money balance number on the monetary record — recollect that an accounting report accounts your advantages, including money — will take after what the bank says you hold in real money. If the QuickBooks accounting report says rather that you're holding $34 million in real money, you'll realize that something is spoiled in Denmark.

Chapter Two: Setting Up

However, before you can begin using QuickBooks, you have to do some direct work. In particular, you have to get ready for the QuickBooks Setup process. And afterward, you have to stroll through the Setup steps. Right now, describe how you do so much stuff.

You have to finish three tasks to prepare for QuickBooks Setup:

Settle on a significant choice about your change date. Set up a preliminary balance as of the change date.

Go on a scavenger chase to gather a lot of stuff that you'll need or discover convenient for the meeting

The major choice

Before you tinker with your PC or the QuickBooks programming, you have to pick the date — the alleged change date — on which you need to start using QuickBooks for your budgetary record keeping.

This choice is immensely significant because the change date that you pick drastically influences both the work you need to do to get QuickBooks running easily and the underlying handiness of the money related data that you gather and record by using QuickBooks.

You have three essential options:

The correct way: You can change over toward the start of your accounting year (which, much of the time, is equivalent to the start of the schedule year). Along these lines is the correct route for two reasons. Initially, changing over toward the start of the year requires a minimal measure of work from you.

Second, it implies that you have all the present year's budgetary data in a single system.

The marginally clumsy way: You can change over toward the start of some between time accounting period (most likely the start of some month or quarter). This methodology works, yet it's marginally clumsy because you need to plug your year-to-date pay and costs numbers from the old system into the new system.

The my-way-or-the-roadway way: You can change over sooner or later other than what I call the correct way and the marginally unbalanced way. In particular, you can decide to change over at whatever point you sprightly well feel like it.

You do a lot of superfluous work for yourself if you adopt this strategy, and you pull out a lot of your hair all the while. Yet, you additionally have the fulfillment of realizing that through it everything, you did it your way — with no assistance from me.

I suggest picking the correct way. What this decision implies is that if it's late in the year — state, October — you simply hold up until January 1 of the following year to change over. If it's still from the get-go in the year, you can retroactively change over as of the start of the year. (If you do this, you have to return and make your money related record-keeping for the initial segment of the present year by using QuickBooks: entering sales, recording buys, etc.)

If it's at some point in the year — state, Memorial Day or later — you likely need to use the somewhat clumsy way. (I'm really going to use the somewhat cumbersome route right now the following section in such a case that you perceive how to change over to QuickBooks by using the marginally clumsy way, you realize how to use both the correct way and the somewhat ungainly way.)

The preliminary balance of the century

After you choose when you need to change over, you need a preliminary balance.

"Yowser," you state. "What's a preliminary balance?" A preliminary balance just accounts for every one of your advantages, liabilities, and proprietor's value account balances just as the year-to-date pay and cost numbers on a predefined date (which, not adventitiously, happens to be the transformation date). You need this information for the QuickBooks Setup process and for some fiddling around that you have to do after you complete the QuickBooks Setup process.

Just to dwell on silly trifles, the preliminary balance should show account balances at the very beginning of the principal day that you'll start using QuickBooks for genuine accounting. If the change date is 1/1/2019, for instance, the preliminary balance needs to show the record balances at one moment past 12 PM on 1/1/2019. This is additionally exactly the same thing as indicating the record balances at the finish of the most recent day that you'll be using the old accounting system — at the end of the day, at precisely 12 PM on 12/31/2016 in case you're changing over to QuickBooks on 1/1/2019.

If your old system is fairly casual (maybe it's a shoebox loaded with receipts), or if it tracks just money (maybe you've been using Quicken), you have to do more work:

To get your money balance: Reconcile your ledger or financial balances (if you have more than one ledger) as of the change date.

To get your accounts receivable balance: Tally all your unpaid client invoices.

To get your other resource account balances: Know what every advantage initially costs. For depreciable fixed resources, you additionally need to give any aggregated devaluation that has been asserted for that advantage. (Amassed deterioration is the complete devaluation that you've just expensed for every advantage.)

To get your obligation account balances: Know the amount you owe on every risk. If you confide in your lenders — the individuals to whom you owe the cash — you may likewise have the option to get this data from their announcements.

You don't have to stress over the proprietor's value accounts. QuickBooks can ascertain your proprietor's value account balances for you, in light of the distinction between your complete resources and your all-out liabilities. This strategy is somewhat messy, and bookkeepers dislike it, yet it's a truly decent trade-off. (If you do have a point by point account balances for your proprietor's value accounts, use these figures — and realize that you're one out of a million.)

In case you're using the marginally unbalanced approach to change over to QuickBooks — at the end of the day if your transformation date is some date other than the start of the accounting year — you additionally need to give year-to-date salary and cost balances. To get your pay, cost of products sold, costs, other pay, and other business ledger balances, you have to figure the year-to-date measure of each record. If you can get this data from your old system, that is super. If not, you have to get it physically. (If you out of nowhere have pictures of yourself sitting at your work area late around evening time, tapping ceaselessly on a ten-key, you're presumably right. Likewise, you presumably additionally need to designate a portion of another Saturday to getting QuickBooks ready for action.)

The mother of all scavenger hunts

Considerably after you choose when you need to change over to QuickBooks and you think of a preliminary balance, you, despite everything, need to gather a lot of extra data. I list these things in the clothing list design. What you need to do is discover so much stuff and afterward heap it up (conveniently) in a major stack beside the PC:

A year ago, government expense form: QuickBooks asks which bureaucratic personal tax document you use to record your assessment form and furthermore gets some information about your citizen ID number. A year ago, the government expense form was the most effortless spot to discover this stuff.

Copies of all your latest state and government finance assessment forms: If you plan the finance for workers, QuickBooks needs to think about the administrative and state finance charge rates that you pay, just like some other stuff.

Copies of all the unpaid invoices that your clients (or customers or patients or whatever) owe you as of the transformation date: I surmise this is likely self-evident, yet the all-out accounts receivable balance appeared on your preliminary balance needs to coordinate the aggregate of the unpaid client invoices.

Copies of every single unpaid bill that you owe your sellers as of the change date: Again, this is most likely self-evident, yet the absolute accounts payable balance appeared on your preliminary balance needs to coordinate the aggregate of the unpaid merchant bills.

A nitty-gritty posting of any stock things you're holding for resale: This list ought to incorporate stock thing descriptions and amounts, yet additionally, the underlying buy costs and the foreseen sales costs. At the end of the day, if you sell porcelain wombats, and you have 1,200 of these wonders in stock, you have to know precisely what you paid for them.

Copies of the earlier year's W-2 articulations, W-4 proclamations for anyone you contracted since the start of the earlier year, point by point data about any finance charge liabilities you owe as of the transformation date, and nitty-gritty data about the finance charge stores you made since the start of the year: You need the data appeared on these forms to satisfactorily and precisely set up the QuickBooks finance include. I would prefer not to panic you; however, this is likely the dreariest piece of setting up QuickBooks.

In case you're retroactively changing over as of the start of the year, you need a list of the considerable number of transactions that have happened since the start of the year: sales, buys, finance transactions, and everything and whatever else: If you do the right-way transformation retroactively, you have to reemerge every one of these transactions into the new system. You really enter the data after you complete the QuickBooks Setup process, which I describe later right now, you should get this data together now, while you're looking for the remainder of the things for this scrounger chase.

Venturing through QuickBooks Setup

After you choose when you need to change over, set up a preliminary balance as of the transformation date, and gather the extra crude information that you need, you're prepared to step through QuickBooks Setup. You have to begin

QuickBooks and afterward stroll through the means.

Beginning QuickBooks

To begin QuickBooks 2019 in Windows 10, click the QuickBooks 2019 tile on the Windows Desktop. Or then again, click the Windows Start window and afterward click the menu decision that prompts QuickBooks. (I pick Start ⇒ All Apps ⇒ QuickBooks ⇒ QuickBooks Enterprise Solutions 17.0.)

If you've begun QuickBooks just because, QuickBooks first reveals to you how it intends to use your Internet association with consistently update the QuickBooks programming. After you click the button that specifies, "Alright, definitely, I'm acceptable with that," QuickBooks shows the No Company Open discourse box (not appeared). Then you click the Create a New Company button so that QuickBooks shows the QuickBooks Setup transaction box with the message. Let's get your business set up rapidly

I should make reference to that the first QuickBooks Setup discourse box recognizes some other alignment choices you can use to begin. The discourse box gives you the Detailed Start choice, for instance, which lets you control the alignment and adjust the organization document. The discourse box likewise gives you the alternative to make another record from an old document. It additionally proposes that you should update from Quicken or some other accounting system. (Essentially, that overhaul implies that you need QuickBooks to take a stab at using your current accounting system's information as a beginning stage.)

Two basic bits of exhortation: Don't tinker with Detailed Setup except if you're an accounting master, and don't endeavor to "redesign" Quicken or some other accounting system's information. It's similarly as simple and normally significantly cleaner to work from a preliminary balance.

Using the Express Setup

QuickBooks 2019 gives you a quick alignment process contrasted and other accounting programming programs and even with old renditions of the QuickBooks programming. Essentially, you fill in some containers and click a few buttons, and presto — you've to a great extent set up QuickBooks. Since I can give you a few hints, distinguish a few alternate routes, and caution you of certain snares to keep away from, I'm giving these bits by bit directions:

1. In the first QuickBooks Setup discourse box, pick Express Setup.

With the first QuickBooks Setup discourse box showed, click the Express Start button. QuickBooks shows the Glad You're Here! Discourse box.

2. Determine the business name.

The name you determine goes on QuickBooks reports and shows up on invoices you send clients. In like manner, you need to use your "genuine" business name. If your business is joined or framed as a restricted obligation organization (LLC), you need to use the correct addition or abbreviation in your name. Try not to use Acme Supplies, for instance, yet Acme Supplies Inc. or, on the other hand, Acme Supplies LLC.

Note: QuickBooks likewise uses the organization name for the QuickBooks information record.

3. Distinguish your industry.

In case you're in the development business, for instance, type development. When you type something in the Industry field, QuickBooks transforms the crate into a drop-down menu indicating the ventures that it perceives. You can pick an industry from this menu (or pick the business that is nearest to your business).

4. Recognize the expense form you record.

Use the Business Type field to determine the expense form that your business accounts. You can click that field and afterward settle on a decision from the menu that QuickBooks gives.

5. Give your Employer Identification Number.

Use the Employer Identification Number (EIN) field to give your business citizen a recognizable proof number. In case you're sole ownership without employees, your assessment ID number might be your Social Security number. In every single other case, your citizen distinguishing proof number is your Employer Identification Number.

6. Give your place of work data.

Use the Business Address fields to give your association's location and contact data. I trust you don't feel bamboozled that I'm not giving you guidelines like "Enter your road address in the Address box" and "Please recall that your phone number goes in the Phone box."

7. Make the QuickBooks information document.

After you give the business contact data mentioned by QuickBooks, click the Create Company button. QuickBooks may show the QuickSetup transaction box, which allows you to name and determine the area of the organization record. You can use the QuickSetup transaction box to roll out these improvements or — my suggestion — just let QuickBooks be QuickBooks and settle on these choices for you. After you click Save, QuickBooks makes the information record it will use to store your money related data. (In certain renditions of QuickBooks, making the document takes a couple of moments.)

When QuickBooks wraps up your document, it shows the Get All the Details into QuickBooks discourse box.

8. Recognize your clients, sellers, and employees.

With the Get All the Details into QuickBooks transaction box showed, click the Add the People You Do Business With button. QuickBooks shows another discourse box that asks, "Perchance, are contact names and addresses put away electronically somewhere else, like Microsoft Outlook or Google Gmail?"

If you do have a contact name and address data put away somewhere else that QuickBooks will recover: Click the fitting window and adhere to the on-screen guidelines.

Something else: Click the Paste from Excel or Enter Manually window and afterward click Continue.

When QuickBooks shows the Add the People You Do Business With transaction box, use the lines of the showed worksheet to describe your clients, sellers, and employees. To enter a contact into the following empty column:

- Select the Customer, Vendor, or Employee choice button (as suitable).

- Describe the contact using the fields gave: Name, Company Name, First Name, Last Name, Email, Phone, etc. Each contact goes in its own column.

- Click the Continue button twice when you wrap up your contacts to come back to the Get All the Details into QuickBooks transaction box.

9. Distinguish the things (the stuff) you sell.

With the Get All the Details into QuickBooks discourse box showed, click the Add the Products and Services You Sell button. QuickBooks shows another transaction box that solicits what kind from stuff you need to describe: administrations, stuff that you track in stock, stuff that is stock however that you don't follow, etc. (Which things QuickBooks accounts relies upon the business that you determine in Step 3.) Click the fitting button.

When QuickBooks shows the Add the Products and Services, You Sell discourse box, use the columns of the showed worksheet to describe an item or administration. For anything, you'll generally enter a name, description, and cost. For certain things, however, you can determine a lot more noteworthy detail than simply this skeletal data. Click the Continue button when you wrap up your items and administrations. QuickBooks may attempt to sell you some additional stuff (for example, Intuit checks), however, don't hesitate to click No Thanks to coming back to the Get All the Details into QuickBooks discourse box.

10. Describe your bank account(s).

With the Get All the Details into QuickBooks discourse box showed, click the Add Your Bank Accounts button. When QuickBooks shows the Add Your Bank Accounts transaction box, use the worksheet to describe each financial balance you use for your business: its name, account number, balance at the transformation date, and the genuine change date. Click the Continue button when you wrap up your financial balances to come back to the Get All the Details into QuickBooks discourse box.

11. Begin working with QuickBooks.

With the Get All the Details into QuickBooks transaction box showed, click the Start Working button. QuickBooks shows the QuickBooks program window. You're finished.

If you didn't enlist during the establishment procedure, eventually, after QuickBooks begins, you see a message box that asks whether you need to enlist QuickBooks. If you don't enlist, you can use the item approximately a couple of times, and afterward — the program buttons up, and you can never again get to your accounts. Possibly you register it, or you can't use it. I don't care for being compelled to accomplish something; however, getting worked up about enrolling QuickBooks is an exercise in futility.

The least complex choice is to enroll when you see that message simply. Here's how: When

QuickBooks shows the message box that asks whether you need to enlist, click the Online button to enlist on the web, or click the Phone button to enlist via telephone. If you go with the Phone alternative, QuickBooks shows another discourse box that gives you a phone number to call and gives a space to you to enter your enlistment number.

The Rest of the Story

In the former passages of this part, I describe how you plan for and afterward step through the QuickBooks Setup process. When QuickBooks Setup is finished, however, you have to deal with three other little employments:

You have to describe in detail your stock, your client receivables, and (if you decided to follow merchant charges you owe) your seller payables.

You have to describe your present business accounts, including any year-to-date income and year-to-date costs that aren't recorded as a feature of getting your client receivables and merchant payables, went into QuickBooks.

If you need to use group premise accounting, you have to make an alteration.

These errands aren't tedious; however, they're the three most entangled undertakings that you have to do to set up QuickBooks.

To set up the stock accounts, you simply recognize the thing that includes you hold in stock, as described in Chapter 3.

To set up your client receivables and (if essential) merchant payables, you first need to enter client invoices that were set up before the transformation date, however, that are as yet uncollected at change, as described in Chapter 4.

Additionally, you may need to enter seller payables that were brought about before the change date; however, that is as yet unpaid at the transformation.

I talk about this stuff more in the following part, so in case you're despite everything OK with doing some more establishment and alignment work, feel free to flip there.

Would it be a good idea for you to Get Your Accountant's Help?

So would it be a good idea for you to find support from your bookkeeper? I don't have the foggiest idea. If you follow my bearings cautiously (both right now the following), and your business budgetary issues aren't fiercely intricate, I figure you can most likely make sense of so much stuff alone.

Having said that, in any case, I recommend that you, at any rate, consider getting your bookkeeper's assistance at this crossroads. Your bookkeeper can improve the employment of offering you guidance that might be explicit to your circumstance. As a rule, your bookkeeper can give you starting preliminary offset sums that concur with your government forms. The individual in question presumably knows your business and can shield you from ruining things, just if you don't follow my headings cautiously.

To make sure you know: One of the things that I (as a CPA) accomplish for my customers is to assist them with setting up QuickBooks. Since I do this, I can give you two or three bits of valuable data about getting a CPA's assistance in setting up:

Your CPA (accepting that the person in question definitely knows QuickBooks) ought to have the option to help you through the alignment procedure in two or three hours, by and large, so the individual in question can do it (or assist you with doing it) a lot quicker than you can without anyone else.

Another (a third) hour or so of coaching from your CPA should imply that you get enough assistance to record all your standard transactions.

With simply this assistance, you can discover how to cover your tabs, receipt clients precisely how you need, and produce reports. I used to pooh-pooh this sort of hand-holding. However, the older (and, I trust, smarter) I get, the more I see that entrepreneurs and accountants profit by this in advance assistance. A touch of arranging and master exhortation at the outset can save you a mess of difficulty later.

Chapter Three: Fundamental Steps to Using Quickbook

QuickBooks Setup (which I talk about at some length in Chapter 2) doesn't prepare QuickBooks totally to use. You likewise need to enter extra data about your items, workers, clients, and sellers (and a bunch of different things) into accounts. Right now, describe how you make and work with these lists. I additionally describe how you tidy up a portion of the accounting chaos created when you enter data into these lists.

The Magic and Mystery of Items

The first QuickBooks show you have to wrap setting up is the Item list — the list of stuff you purchase and sell. Before you begin adding to your Item list, notwithstanding, I have to reveal to you that QuickBooks isn't brilliant about its perspective on what you purchase and sell. It imagines that anything you stick on a business receipt or a buy request is something you're selling.

If you sell bright espresso cups, for instance, you likely figure (and effectively so), you have to include descriptions of every one of these things to the Item list. If you add cargo charges to a receipt, in any case, QuickBooks imagines that you include another mug. And, if you add sales expense to a receipt, well, learn to expect the unexpected. QuickBooks again believes that you contain another mug.

This wacky meaning of things is confounding from the start. In any case, simply recollect a specific something, and you'll be alright. You aren't the person who's dumb: QuickBooks is. No, I'm not saying that QuickBooks is an awful program. It's an excellent accounting program and an incredible device. I'm saying that QuickBooks is just a simple PC program; it is anything but a human-made reasoning system. It doesn't get on the little nuances of business —, for example, the way that even though you charge clients for cargo, you aren't generally in the delivery business.

Every section in the receipt or buy request — the mugs that you sell, the subtotal, the markdown, the cargo charges, and the business charge — is a thing. Indeed, I realize this alignment is strange, yet becoming acclimated to the wackiness now makes the discussions that follow a lot more obvious.

Including things you may incorporate invoices

You may have included a few things as a component of QuickBooks Setup; however, you'll need to realize how to add some other required things and how to add new things. To include a receipt or buy request things to the Item list, follow these means:

1. Pick Lists ⇒ Item List.

If QuickBooks asks whether you need to set up various things, designate "No chance, man." QuickBooks then shows the Item List window.

2. Click the Item button at the base of the Item List window and afterward select New starting from the drop list.

3. Classify the thing.

Select a thing type from the Type drop-down list. The Item list that you see relies upon the sort of business you disclosed to QuickBooks you were in when you set up the program, so use the accompanying as an example; the sum and kind of things that you need rely upon the business you're in. Select one of the accompanying thing types by clicking its name in the list:

Administration: Select this sort if you charge for help, for example, an hour of work or a fixed work.

Stock Part: Select this sort if what you sell is something that you purchase from another person, and you need to follow your property of the thing. If you sell gizmos that you buy from maker Thingamajigs Amalgamated, for instance, you determine the thing type as Inventory Part.

Stock Assembly: Select this sort if what you sell is something that you make from other Inventory things. At the end of the day, if you purchase crude materials or different parts and then amass these things to make your completed item, the finished item is an Inventory Assembly thing.

Non-Inventory Part: Select this sort if what you sell is something that you would prefer not to follow as stock. (You typically don't use this thing type for items that you sell, incidentally. Instead, you use it for things that you purchase for the business and need to remember to buy orders.)

Other Charge: Select this thing type for things, for example, cargo and taking care of charges that you remember for invoices.

Subtotal: This thing type includes everything before you subtract any markdown, include the business charge, etc.

Group: Use this thing type to enter a lot of things (which are on the list) at once. This thing is a decent timesaver. If you generally sell sets of things, for instance, you don't need to indicate those things independently every time you write a receipt.

Markdown: This thing type ascertains an add up to be subtracted from a subtotal.

Installment: This choice is wacky. If your receipt some of the time incorporates a passage that diminishes the receipt complete — client stores at the hour of the offer, for instance — select this thing type. Notwithstanding, if this thing type befuddles you, simply overlook it.

Sales Tax Item: Select this thing type for the business charge that you remember for the receipt.

Sales Tax Group: This thing type is like the Group thing type, yet you use it just for sales charges that are gathered in one transaction and owed to various offices.

4. Type a thing number or name.

Press the Tab key or use your mouse to tap the Item Name/Number content box underneath the Type drop-down list, then type a short description of the thing.

5. (Discretionary) Make the thing a sub-item.

If you need to work with sub-items — things that show up inside different things — select the Sub item Of checkbox and use the comparing drop-down list to determine the parent thing to which a sub-item has a place.

6. Describe the thing in more detail.

Move the cursor to the Description content box, and type a description. This description then shows up in the receipt. Note that if you indicated the thing type as Inventory Part in Step 3, you see two description content boxes: Description on Purchase Transactions and Description on Sales Transactions. The buy description shows up in buy orders, and the business description shows up in sales invoices.

7. If the thing type is Service, Non-Inventory Part, or Other Charge, reveal to QuickBooks the amount to charge for the thing, regardless of whether the thing is dependent upon sales assessment. Which

salary record to use for following the pay that you get from selling the thing.

For a Service type, use the Rate content box to determine the value you charge for one unit of the administration. If you charge continuously, for instance, the rate is the charge for an hour of administration. If you charge for work, for example, a fixed work or the fulfillment of a particular assignment, the rate is the charge for the job or errand.

For a Non-Inventory Part type, use the Price content box to indicate the sum you charge for the thing.

For the Other Charge type, use the Amount or % content box, which replaces the Rate content box, to determine the sum you charge for the thing. You can type a quantity, for example, 20 for $20.00, or you can type a rate. If you type a rate, QuickBooks ascertains the Other Charge Amount as the price increased by the first thing that appeared on the receipt.

8. If the thing type is Inventory Part, reveal to QuickBooks the amount to charge for the stock part, how much the stock part expenses, and which

salary record to use for following the item sales pay.

For an Inventory Part thing type, QuickBooks shows the New Item window. You use the additional fields that this beautiful adaptation of the window showcases to record the accompanying data:

The description of Purchase Transactions: Describe the part. This shows up in the reports (for example, buy arranges) that you use when you purchase things for your stock.

Cost: Specify the average expense per unit of the things that you presently have. This field goes about as the default rate when you enter the thing in a buy transaction.

Pinions Account: Specify the record that you need QuickBooks to use for following this current thing's cost when you sell it. (QuickBooks recommends the COGS, or loss of merchandise sold account. If you've made different accounts for your COGS, select the suitable record.)

Favored Vendor: Specify your first decision when requesting the thing for your business. (If the seller isn't in your Vendor list, QuickBooks requests that you include it. If you state, "No doubt,

I would like to include it," QuickBooks shows the Add Vendor window, which you can use to describe the merchant.)

The description of Sales Transactions: Type a description of the thing that you need to show up in reports (invoices, etc.) that your clients see. QuickBooks proposes a similar description that you used in the Description on Purchase Transactions content box as a default.

Sales Price: Enter the sum that you charge for the thing.

Expense Code: Indicate whether the thing is burdened.

Pay Account: Specify the record that you need QuickBooks to use for following the salary from the offer of the part. This is presumably the Merchandise Income or Sales account. You commonly use the Merchandise Income record to monitor discount (nontaxable) sales and the Sales record to follow retail sales.

Resource Account: Specify the other current resource account that you need QuickBooks to use for following this Inventory thing's worth.

Reorder Point: Specify the most minimal stock amount of this thing that can stay before you request more. When the stock level drops to this amount, QuickBooks adds a suggestion to the Reminders list, telling you that you have to reorder the thing. (To see the Reminders list, pick Edit ⇒ Preferences, select Reminders, and afterward select the Show Reminders List When Opening Company File box on the My Preferences tab.)

On Hand: If you're setting up a thing just because as a significant aspect of setting up QuickBooks, set this field to the physical mean the thing at the transformation date. Something else, leave this field set to zero.

Complete Value: Leave this field set to zero as well.

As Of: Enter the present date.

9. If the thing type is Inventory Assembly, disclose to QuickBooks which COGS and pay record to use for following the thing, the amount to charge for the stock get together, and how to manufacture the thing from other segment Inventory things.

Note: The Inventory Assembly thing is accessible in QuickBooks Premier and Enterprise, however not in Simple Start or QuickBooks Pro.

For an Inventory Assembly thing type, QuickBooks shows the New Item window. You use the additional fields that this extraordinary variant of the window showcases to record the accompanying data:

Gear-teeth Account: Specify the record that you need QuickBooks to use for following this present thing's cost when you sell it. (QuickBooks recommends the COGS account. If you've made different accounts for your COGS, select the proper record.)

Description: Type a description of the thing that you need to show up in archives that your clients see, for example, invoices.

Sales Price: Enter the sum that you charge for the thing.

Duty Code: Indicate whether the thing is exhausted.

Pay Account: Specify the record that you need QuickBooks to use for following the pay from the offer of the part. This is presumably the Merchandise Sales or Sales Income account. You regularly use the Merchandise Sales record to track offers of substantial things (stock, at the end of the day) and the Sales Income record to follow whatever else.

Bill of Materials: Use the Bill of Materials list to recognize the part things and the amounts expected to make the stock groups.

Resource Account: Specify the other current resource account that you need QuickBooks to use for following this Inventory thing's worth.

Construct Point: Specify the most reduced stock amount of this thing that can stay before you make more. When the stock level drops to this amount, QuickBooks adds a suggestion to the Reminders list, telling you that you have to make a more significant amount of the thing.

On Hand: If you're setting up a thing just because as a significant aspect of setting up QuickBooks, set this field to the physical mean the thing at the change date. Something else, leave this field set to zero.

All out Value: If you enter a worth other than zero in the On Hand field, set the total worth sum at the expense of the things you're holding. Something else, leave this field set to zero.

As Of: Enter the transformation date in the as of content box in case you're describing something as a component of getting QuickBooks set up.

Something else, enter the present date.

10. If the thing type is Sales Tax Item, reveal to QuickBooks what sales charge rate to charge and what government office to pay.

Enter the business charge rate in the appropriate box and the state (or the city or other assessment office name) in the proper box:

Sales Tax Name and Description: Specify further subtleties for later recognizable proof.

Expense Rate: Specify the business charge rate as a rate.

Assessment Agency: Name the state or neighborhood charge office that gathers all the loot that you transmit. If the assessment organization isn't on the list, you can include it by choosing Add New starting from the drop list.

11. If the thing type is Payment, describe the installment strategy and how you need QuickBooks to deal with the installment.

You use installment things to record an upfront installment made when the receipt is made to decrease the last funds to be paid from the client later. Note: Retainers and advance stores are dealt with unexpectedly.

12. Click OK or Next when you're done.

When you complete the process of describing one thing, click OK to add the thing to the list and come back to the Item List window. Click Next to add the thing to the list and keep the New Item window onscreen with the goal that you can include more things.

13. If you included another Inventory thing, record the acquisition of the thing.

After you wrap up any new Inventory things, you have to make another transaction to arrange the acquisition of the things (except if they just appeared one morning on your doorstep).

Making other wacky things for invoices

In the previous segment, I won't describe all the things that you can include. You can make a Subtotal thing to ascertain the subtotal of the things you list in a receipt, for instance. (You, for the most part, need this subtotal when you need to compute sales charge on the receipt's things.) You should make other wacky things for your invoices also, for example, limits. I describe these extraordinary sorts of things in the following, hardly any segments.

Making Subtotal things to stick subtotals on invoices

You have to include a Subtotal thing if you ever need to apply a rebate to a progression of things on a receipt. To add a Subtotal thing to your Item list, pick Lists ⇒ Item List, click the Item button, and select New starting from the drop list. This job shows the New Item window — a similar window I show a few times before now. Indicate the thing type as Subtotal and afterward give a thing name, (for example, Subtotal).

Making Group things to cluster stuff you sell together

You can make a thing that puts one line on a receipt that is a blend of a few different things. To include a Group thing, show the New Item window and indicate the thing type as Group.

In the New Item window, use the Item/Description/Qty list box to list everything remembered for the groups. When you click a thing line in the Item/Description/Qty list box, QuickBooks places a down button at the correct finish of the Item segment. Click this button to open a drop-down list of things. (If the file is more extended than can be appeared, you can use the parchment bar on the option to go here and there the list.) If you select the Print Items in the Group checkbox, QuickBooks accounts for all the things in the groups in invoices. (On account of the mugs, invoices list the individual blue, red, and yellow mugs as opposed to posting the group's name, for example, Mug Set.)

Making Discount things to add limits to invoices

You can make a thing that ascertains a markdown and sticks the rebate in a receipt in different detail.

To add a Discount thing to the list, show the New Item window, indicate the thing type as Discount, and give a thing name or number and description.

Use the Amount or % content box to indicate how the markdown is determined if the rebate is a set sum (for example, $50.00), type the sum. If the refund is determined as a rate, enter the price, including the percent image. When you enter a rate, QuickBooks ascertains the markdown sum as the rate increased by the former thing appeared in the receipt. (If you need to apply the markdown to a group's of things, you have to use a Subtotal thing and tail it with the rebate).

Use the Account drop-down list to indicate the business ledger that you need to use to follow the expense of the limits you offer.

Use the Tax Code drop-down list to indicate whether the rebate gets determined previously or after any sales charges are determined. (This choice shows up just if you demonstrated during QuickBooks Setup that you charge sales charge.)

If you have to gather sales expense, and you didn't set up this capacity in QuickBooks Setup, follow these means:

1. Pick Edit ⇒ Preferences.

The Preferences transaction box shows up.

2. Click the Sales Tax symbol in the list on the left, click the Company Preferences tab, and afterward

select the Yes choice button in the Do You Charge Sales Tax territory.

3. Include the Sales Tax item(s) to your Item list.

4. Click the Add Sales Tax Item button.

When QuickBooks shows the New Item transaction box (not appeared), enter a name for the business charge in the Sales Tax Name box, the business charge rate in the Tax Rate box, and the state office to which you dispatch the business charge in the Tax Agency box. Click OK twice when you've done this to close the New Item discourse box and the Preferences transaction box.

Making Sales Tax Group things to clump sales charges

Sales Tax Groups empower you to bunch a few sales imposes that you should charge as one duty with the goal that they show up as a separate sales charge in the receipt.

Consolidating the duties is fundamental — or if nothing else conceivable — when you should charge, say, a 6.5 percent state sales charge, a 1.7 percent region sales charge, and a 0.4 percent city sales charge. However, you need to give one full 8.6 percent sales charge in the receipt.

To include a Sales Tax Group thing, show the New Item window and afterward indicate the thing type as Sales Tax Group.

Use the Tax Item/Rate/Tax Agency/Description list box to list different sales charge things that you need to remember for the groups. When you click a thing line in the list box, QuickBooks places a down button at the correct finish of the Tax Item segment. You can click this button to open a drop-down list of Sales Tax things.

Editing things

If you commit an error, you can change any bit of thing data by showing the Item List window and double-tapping the thing so that QuickBooks shows the Edit Item window, which you can use to make changes

Adding Employees to Your Employee List

If you do finance in QuickBooks, or if you track sales by employees, you have to describe every worker. Representing employees is pretty darn simple. Pick the Employees ⇒ Employee Center direction to show the Employee Center window. Then click the New Employee button that shows up directly over the list in the upper left corner of the screen to have QuickBooks show the New Employee window.

The New Employee window is quite direct, isn't that so? You simply fill in the fields to describe the worker.

Lesser PC book essayists most likely would give bit by bit descriptions of how you move the cursor to the First Name content box and type the individual's first name, how you move the cursor to the following content box, type something there, etc. Not me. No chance. I realize that you can tell just by looking at this window that everything you do is click a book box and type the conspicuous piece of data. Isn't that so?

When you discharge an employee, it's imperative to enter the discharge date for the worker on the Employment Info tab after you write that last check. (To change to another tab, click the tab's name. Click Employment Info to show the Employment Info tab, for instance.) This way, when you process finance, later on, you can't incidentally pay the previous worker.

Concerning the Type field alternative on the Employment Info tab, most workers likely fit the standard classification. In case you're questioning whether an employee meets the rules for corporate official, statutory worker, or proprietor, see the Circular E distribution from the IRS. Also, rest tight.

The Address and Contact tab give boxes to you to gather and store address data. The Additional Info tab empowers you to make adjustable fields if you need to keep data that isn't secured by the QuickBooks default fields — most loved shading and that sort of thing. Once more, what you have to do on this tab is genuinely direct.

Incidentally, if you disclosed to QuickBooks that you need to do finance, QuickBooks prompts you to enter the data it needs to figure things like government and state annual expenses, finance charges. And excursion pays using boxes and windows that show up on the Payroll Info and Worker's Comp tabs.

After you wrap up an employee, click OK to add the worker to the list and come back to the Employee List window, or click Next to add the employee to the list and include more employees.

You can likewise inactivate an employee from your list if the list begins to get jumbled with the names of employees who never again work for you. Find out about inactivating things, employees, clients, and merchants in the close by "Inactivating list things" sidebar. I prescribe standing by to inactivate previous employees until after the year is done, and the W-2 forms have been printed.

Clients Are Your Business

Here's how you add clients to your Customer list:

1. Pick Customers ⇒ Customer Center.

The Customer Center window shows up.

2. Click the New Customer and Job window and afterward click New Customer.

QuickBooks shows the Address Info tab of the New Customer window. Use this window to describe the client in however much detail as could reasonably be expected.

3. Type the client's name.

Enter the name of the client as you need it to show up in the Customer list. Note this is the name that you use to allude to the client inside QuickBooks, so you can curtail or abbreviate the name if you need it. If IBM Corp. is your client, for instance, you may enter just IBM in the Customer Name content box.

4. Determine the aggregate of the client's unpaid invoices by using the Opening Balance content box.

Move the cursor to the Opening Balance content box, and type the aggregate sum owed by the client on the change date.

5. Enter the present date in the as of content box.

6. Enter the full organization name in the Company Name content box.

7. (Discretionary) Enter the name of your contact, alongside other relevant data.

Move the cursor to the Full Name content boxes, and enter the client contact individual's first name, center introductory, and last name. You can likewise open the contact's authentic situation in the Job Title content box.

8. Give phone, fax, and email contact subtleties.

Feel free to fill in the phone number, fax, site, and email content boxes.

9. Enter the billing address.

You can use the Invoice/Bill To content box to give the client's billing address. QuickBooks copies the Company and Contact names to the primary lines of the billing address, so you have to enter just the location. To move from the finish of one line to the beginning of the following, press Enter.

10. Enter the transportation address.

You can use the Ship-To content box to give the client's transportation address. Click the Copy button to copy the billing address to the Ship To field. If the delivery address contrasts from the Bill to address, permanently open the Ship to drop-down list, click Add New, and afterward enter the transportation address data a similar way that you enter the Bill to address. You can include various transportation addresses. After you include a delivery address for a client, you can choose the transportation address from the Ship to the drop-down list.

11. (Discretionary) Click the Payment Settings tab and record more information.

You can use the containers on the Payment Settings tab to record bits of client data, for example, the record number that ought to be incorporated with any installments. You can likewise record installment related data, for example, the client's credit farthest points and charge card data.

12. (Discretionary) Click the Sales Tax Settings tab and determine the client's business charge rate.

You can use the crates on the Sales Tax Setting tab (not appeared) to store the suitable sales charge thing and rate. And to record the client's resale declaration number if that is required because occasionally, you offer things to a client that aren't dependent upon sales charge.

13. (Discretionary) Click the Additional Info tab and record more information.

You can use this tab to describe the client in more detail. You can, for instance, sort the client through the Customer Type drop-down list box. (QuickBooks at first recommends using the client types From Advertisement, Referral, Retail, and wholesale; however, you can tap the Add New section in the list box to include your client types.)

You can use the Rep field to record the salesman relegated to a client. (See "The Sales Rep list" later right now more data.)

You can likewise tap the Define Fields button to show discourse boxes you use to make fields for groups your own redid bits of extra data. (For some time, I used to use a custom domain to record the showcasing effort that procured a customer or client, and that additional piece of information gave excellent understanding into which promoting and publicizing endeavors conveyed high returns and which didn't.)

14. (Discretionary) Click the Job Info tab to include explicit employment data.

Since you're making another client account, not invoicing by employments, I clarify this progression in the following area. In case you're the "can hardly wait" type, don't hesitate to investigate. You can add a particular job to the new client's data.

15. Save the client data by clicking, OK.

When you wrap up a client, you can save it by clicking OK to add the client to the list and afterward come back to the Customer Center window.

It's Just a Job

In QuickBooks, you can follow invoices by the client or by client and employment. This may sound screwy, however a few organizations receipt clients (maybe a few times) for explicit employments.

Take the instance of a development subcontractor who does foundation work for a bunch of manufacturers of single-family homes. This development subcontractor likely invoices his clients by employment, and he invoices every client a few times for a similar job. He invoices Poverty Rock Builders for the establishment work at 1113 Birch Street when he pours the balance, for instance, and afterward again when he lays the square. At 1028 Fairview, a similar foundation work takes more than one receipt, as well.

To set up occupations for clients, you first need to describe the clients (as I clarify in the former segment). Then follow these means:

1. Pick Customers ⇒ Customer Center.

QuickBooks shows the Customer Center window.

2. Right-click, the client for whom you need to set up an occupation, pick Add Job from the logical menu that shows up, and click the Add Job tab.

QuickBooks shows the New Job window (appeared in Figure 3-11). You use this window to describe the job. A lot of the data right now in the receipt.

3. Include the job name.

The cursor is in the Job Name content box. Simply type the name of the job or task.

4. (Discretionary) if you're following the client's balances by work, enter the employment opportunity's balance.

Move the cursor to the Opening Balance content box, and type the aggregate sum owed by the client for the job you're describing on the change date.

5. Enter the present date in the as of content box.

6. Distinguish the client.

If you chose an inappropriate client in Step 2, take a look at the Customer drop-down list. Does it name the right client? If not, activate the drop-down menu and select the right client.

7. (Discretionary) Name your contact and fill in other significant data.

You can enter the name of your contact and elective contact in the Full Name content boxes. QuickBooks consequently fills in the organization name, complete name, and receipt/bill to fields if that data is accessible for the client you are carrying out the responsibility for. You most likely don't should be told this, yet fill in the Phone, Fax,

Email, and Website content boxes just with the goal that you have that data close by.

8. Enter the job's billing address.

You can use the Invoice/Bill To content box to give the client's job billing address. Since the chances are acceptable that the job billing address is equivalent to the client billing address, QuickBooks copies the billing address from the Customer list. However, if need be, make changes.

9. Select the Ship-To address.

You can use the Ship-To content box to give the job's transportation address. Click the Copy button if the transportation address is equivalent to the Invoice/Bill To address.

10. Click the Payment Settings tab and describe the client's installment game plans.

Using the Payment Settings tab (not appeared), for instance, you can record a record number and favored installment technique. You can set the client's credit limit by using the Credit Limit box. And, you can store Mastercard installment data for clients who need you to keep their card numbers on record.

11. (Enormously discretionary) Click the Additional Info tab and sort the job.

You can use the Customer Type drop-down list of the Additional Info tab (not appeared) to set the job type. The primary starting sorts in the default list are From Advertisement, Referral, Retail, and Wholesale. You can make different sorts by picking Add New from the Customer Type drop-down list (so that QuickBooks shows the New Customer Type discourse box) and afterward filling in the spaces.

12. (Discretionary) Click the Job Info tab and include explicit occupation data.

You can use the Job Status drop-down list to pick None, Pending, Awarded, In Progress, Closed, or Not Awarded, whichever is generally proper. The Start Date is (I realize that this one is difficult to accept) the day you start the job. As anybody most likely is aware, the Projected End Date and the End Date aren't the equivalents.

Try not to fill at last Date until the job is wrapped up. The Job Description field can contain any supportive data you can fit in one line, and Job Type is an additional field you can use. (If you do use this field, you can include a new position type by picking Add New from the Job Type list.)

13. Save the job data by clicking, OK.

Adding Vendors to Your Vendor List

Adding sellers to your Vendor list works a similar fundamental route as adding clients to your Customer list. Here's how to take care of business:

1. Pick Vendors ⇒ Vendor Center or click the Vendors symbol at the highest point of the screen.

QuickBooks shows the Vendor Center window. Alongside posting your merchants, it accounts for any business charge organizations that you distinguished as a significant aspect of setting up Sales Tax things.

2. Click the New Vendor window and afterward pick the New Vendor direction from the menu that shows up.

You use this window to describe the merchants and all their little eccentricities.

3. Enter the merchant name.

The cursor is now in the Vendor Name content box. You should simply type the merchant's name as you need it to show up in the Vendor list. If you need to list your sellers by organization name, enter the organization name. To show them by the first or last name of the agent, enter one of these names. Simply recall that the list is going to sort, one after another in order or numerically, by the data you enter right now, by the information that tails it.

4. (Discretionary) Enter the name of your contact.

Fill in the Full Name content boxes with the client contact's first name, center beginning, and last name. You can likewise supply a title for the contact individual.

5. (Discretionary) Enter the seller's phone and email address and, if accessible, the fax number and site addresses.

You can change the names used for the phone number boxes by picking some other descriptions from their drop-down accounts. Furthermore, do take note that the window additionally has an Other one book box so you can record some other piece of distracting data — may be the contact's weight.

6. Enter the location to which you should mail checks.

You can use the Address Details Billed From and Shipped From content boxes to give the merchants tend to data. QuickBooks copies the Company and Contact names to the primary line of the location, so you have to enter just the road address, city, state, and postal district. To move from the finish of one line to the beginning of the following, press Enter.

7. (Discretionary) Check the default Payment Settings tabs data.

Click the Payment Settings tab to find a good pace of boxes that lets you record the merchant's record number, seller installment terms, the correct name to print on the check, and as far as possible.

8. (Discretionary) Check the default Tax Settings.

You can tap the Tax Settings tab to find a good pace of boxes that lets you record the merchant's assessment distinguishing proof number and show whether the seller ought to get a 1099 data expense form from you toward the year's end.

9. (Discretionary) Provide the default accounts to use with a seller.

You can tap the Account Settings tab to show a shortlist of accounts that QuickBooks will use to prefill account number fields when you enter a bill from the seller.

10. (Discretionary) Click the Additional Info tab and order the seller.

The Additional Info tab at first gives only a Vendor Type drop-down list that you can use to order the seller as an advisor, specialist co-op, provider, or expense organization. You can, nonetheless, put custom fields on the tab by tapping the Define Fields button.

11. Type 0 (zero) in the Opening Balance content box.

You commonly would prefer not to enter the sum you owe the merchant; you do that later when you take care of your tabs. However, in case you're using the group's premise representing your costs (which just implies that your accounting system considers charges costs when you get the bill, not when you take care of the tab). You have to reveal to QuickBooks what sums you owe merchants at the transformation date. You can do that most effectively by entering opening balances for merchants in the Opening Balance box as you set up a seller in the Vendor list.

12. Enter the transformation date in the as of date field.

What you're doing here, coincidentally, is giving the date on which the worth appeared in the Opening Balance content box is right.

13. Save the seller data by clicking, OK.

This progression adds the seller to the list and returns you to the Vendor Center window.

The Other Lists

All through the previous areas, I cover practically all the most significant accounts. A couple of others I haven't discussed at this point are Fixed Asset, Price Level, Billing Rate Level, Sales Tax Code, Classes, Other Names, Sales Rep, Customer Type, Vendor Type, Job Type, Terms, Customer Messages, Payment Method, Ship Via, Vehicle, and Memorized Transactions. I don't give pass up blow descriptions of how you use these lists since you don't generally require them.

The different QuickBooks accounts are commonly more than satisfactory. You can ordinarily use the standard accounts as is without building different accounts.

To make sure I don't leave you stranded, in any case, I need to give you down to business descriptions of these different accounts and what they do.

The Fixed Asset Item list

If you purchase fixed resources — things, for example, vehicles, different household items, random hunks of hardware, etc. — someone should follow this stuff in a list. Why? You have to have this data readily available (or at your bookkeeper's fingertips) to ascertain devaluation. Also, if you later discard something, you need this data to figure the increase or misfortune on the offer of the thing.

Consequently, QuickBooks incorporates a Fixed Asset list.

Note: I should reveal to you that your CPA or duty bookkeeper, as of now, has such a list that the person in question has been keeping up for you. Like, don't as well, thoroughly blow a gasket since this is the principal you've found out about this fixed-resources business.

The Price Level list

On the first occasion, when I experienced the QuickBooks Price Level component, I was woefully confounded about how it functioned. I'm still somewhat confounded — not about how the element functions, yet about who'd genuinely need to use it. However, hell, what do I know? Here's the alignment: Price levels empower you to change a thing cost as you're making a receipt. You can make a cost level that builds the expense for something by 20 percent, for instance, and you make a value level that diminishes the expense for something by 10 percent. You alter a cost by choosing a value level from the Price field of a receipt. (This may not bode well until you see the Create Invoices window.

The Billing Rate Levels list

The Billing Rate Levels list lets you manufacture a list of custom costs for administration things as opposed to using a standard rate for a specific assistance thing. You then use billing rate levels when you receipt a client for administrations.

The Sales Tax Code list

The Sales Tax Code list, which shows up if you turn on the Sales Tax alternative, just keeps up a list of offers charge codes. These business charge codes, when used in a receipt or bill, disclose to QuickBooks whether things are assessable.

The Class list

Classes empower you to arrange transactions by office or area, for instance, with the goal that you can follow inclines and survey execution across parts of your business. Classes are cool (truly cool), yet they add another measurement to the accounting model that you use in QuickBooks, so I'm not going to describe them here. I ask you — nay, I implore you — to get settled with how the remainder of QuickBooks functions before you start messing about with classes. Here are only a bunch of helpful goodies if you need to use classes:

You may need to turn on the QuickBooks Class Tracking highlight. To do this, pick Edit ⇒ Preferences, click the Accounting symbol, click the Company Preferences tab, and select the Use Class Tracking checkbox.

Note: The Class confine shows up information passage windows simply after you turn on Class Tracking.

To show the Class list, pick Lists ⇒ Class List.

To add classes to the Class list, show the Class List window (pick Lists ⇒ Class List), right-click the window, pick New to show the New Class window, and afterward fill in the spaces.

To label transactions as falling into a specific class — invoices, checks, charges, diary passages, etc. — select the proper class from the Class list box.

Coincidentally, one other point: Before you go off and begin using classes to muddle your accounting, ensure that you can't get what you need by expanding your graph of accounts.

The Other Names list

QuickBooks gives an Other Names list that functions as a watered-down, weak Vendor and Employee list mix. You can write checks to individuals named right now list; however, you can't do whatever else. You can't make invoices or buy orders for them, for instance, and you don't get any of the other data that you need to gather for merchants or representatives.

The Sales Rep list

You can make a list of the agents you work with and afterward demonstrate which salesperson offers to a client or produces a deal. To do this, pick

Lists ⇒ Customer and Vendor Profile Lists ⇒ Sales Rep. When you choose this direction, QuickBooks shows the Sales Rep List window, which accounts for all the salesmen. To include salespeople, click the Sales Rep button, select New starting from the drop list, and afterward fill in the window that QuickBooks shows.

Client, Vendor, and Job Types list

You can make alignments of client types, seller types, and employment types and afterward use these lists to sort client, merchant, and occupation data. This is most likely nothing unexpected; however, to do this, you have to use the appropriate direction:

Accounts ⇒ Customer and Vendor Profile Lists ⇒ Customer Type List Lists ⇒ Customer and Vendor Profile Lists ⇒ Vendor Type List Lists ⇒ Customer and Vendor Profile Lists ⇒ Job Type List

When you pick one of these directions, QuickBooks shows the proper List window, which accounts for all the Customer types, Vendor types, or Job types. To include types, click the Type button, select New starting from the drop list, and afterward fill in the window that QuickBooks shows.

How you use any of these kinds of accounts relies upon your business. In a circumstance where you need to sort or isolate clients, sellers, or employments in some strange way, use the Customer Type, Vendor Type, or Job Type list.

The Terms list

QuickBooks keeps up a Terms list, which you use to indicate what installment terms are accessible. To include terms, pick Lists ⇒ Customer and Vendor Profile Lists ⇒ Terms List. When you choose this direction, QuickBooks shows the Terms List window. To add more terms, click the Terms button, select New starting from the drop list, and afterward fill in the window that QuickBooks shows.

The Customer Message list

This list is another minor player in the QuickBooks dramatization. You can stick messages at the base of invoices if you first sort the message in the Customer Message list. QuickBooks gives a bunch of standard messages: thank you, merry Christmas, mean individuals suck, etc. You can include more messages by picking Lists ⇒ Customer, and Vendor Profile Lists ⇒ Customer

Message List. When QuickBooks shows the Customer Message List window, click its Customer Message window and select New.

Then use the New Customer Message window that QuickBooks presentations to make another message.

The Payment Method list

Presently, this will be a major astonishment. (I'm merely joking.) QuickBooks gives descriptions of the typical installment strategies. You can add to these by picking Lists ⇒ Customer, and Vendor Profile Lists ⇒ Payment Method. When you select this order, QuickBooks shows the lost city of Atlantis. Alright, not so much. QuickBooks shows the Payment Method window. To include more techniques —, for example, PayPal — click the Payment Method button, select New starting from the drop list, and afterward fill in the window that QuickBooks shows.

The Ship Via list

QuickBooks gives descriptions of typical transportation strategies. These descriptions are likely totally satisfactory. If you have to include more, notwithstanding, you can do as such by picking Lists ⇒ Customer and Vendor Profile Lists ⇒ Ship Via. When you select this direction, QuickBooks shows the Ship Via List window, which accounts for all the transportation strategies that you or QuickBooks said are accessible. To include more plans, click the Shipping Method button, select New starting from the drop list, and afterward fill in the window that QuickBooks shows. Companions, it doesn't get a lot simpler than this.

The Vehicle list

QuickBooks gives a Vehicle list that you can use to keep up a list of business vehicles. To see the Vehicle list, pick Lists ⇒ Customer, and Vendor Profile Lists ⇒ Vehicle List. When you choose this order, QuickBooks shows the Vehicle List window, which accounts for all the vehicles that you recently said are accessible. To distinguish new cars, click the Vehicle button, select New starting from the drop list, and afterward fill in the window that QuickBooks shows.

To record vehicle mileage inside QuickBooks, pick Company ⇒ Enter Vehicle Mileage. Then use the window that QuickBooks presentations to recognize the vehicle, the excursion length in miles, the outing date, and a touch of other outing related data.

The Memorized Transaction list

The Memorized Transaction list isn't generally a list. In any event, dislike different accounts that I describe right now. The Memorized Transaction list is a list of accounting transactions — invoices, charges, checks, buy orders, etc. — that you've asked QuickBooks to remember. To show the Memorized Transaction list, pick Lists ⇒ Memorized Transaction List.

You can have QuickBooks retain transactions so you can rapidly record them later or even put them on a timetable for repeating use. This element can save time for deals that are, to a great extent, indistinguishable each time you enter them and that you enter consistently.

The Reminders list

Here's a file that isn't available from the Lists menu. QuickBooks monitors a lot of stuff that it realizes you have to screen. If you pick Company ⇒ Reminders, QuickBooks shows the Reminders window. Here, you consider such to be as invoices and watches that should be printed, stock things you most likely should reorder, etc.

Arranging Lists

To arrange a list, you should be in single-client mode. Here are a few different ways that you can sort out your checklist:

To move a thing and all its subitems: Click the diamond adjacent it and afterward, drag it up or down the list to another area.

To make a subitem its own thing: Click the jewel close to the thing and afterward drag it to one side.

To make a thing a subitem: Move the thing so it's legitimately beneath the thing you need it to fall under. Then click the precious stone close to the thing and drag it to one side.

To order a list: Click the Name button at the highest priority on the list window. QuickBooks orders your list of clients, sellers, accounts, etc. in both a to z request and inverts Z to A request.

Printing Lists

You can print client, merchant, and representative accounts by tapping the Print button at the highest point of the particular Center screen for the sort of show you pick. The list is among the alternatives accessible to print in a drop-down menu.

You can print an ordinary list by showing the menu, tapping the button in the base left corner of the list window, and afterward picking Print List. Regularly, in any case, the perfect approach to print a list is to print a list report. You can make, redo, and print a list report by picking Reports ⇒ List and afterward picking the file that you need to print. You can likewise make one of a bunch of list reports by tapping the Reports button in the list window and picking a report from the spring up menu.

Click the Activities button in a list window to rapidly get to usual exercises related to the things in that list, or click Reports to quickly get to regular reports identified with the things in the list.

Trading List Items to Your Word Processor

If you use QuickBooks to store the names and addresses of your clients, sellers, and workers, you can make a book record of the contact data for these individuals. Then you can trade this record to another application, for example, a word processor, to make reports that utilization this data.

To send out list data to a book document, click the button in the base left corner of the list window, and pick Print List. When QuickBooks shows the Print discourse box, select the File choice button, click Print, and give a filename when provoked.

Managing the Chart of Accounts List

I held back something special for later. After you complete setting up your lists, you, despite everything, need to settle one list: Chart of Accounts. The Chart of Accounts list just accounts for the accounts you and QuickBooks use to follow pay and costs, resources, liabilities, and value.

This progression is somewhat of an entertaining one; however, because a lot of Chart of Accounts stuff is as of now set up, you're only finishing it. Ordinarily, this comprises of two or perhaps three separate steps: describing client balances, describing merchant balances, and entering the remainder of the preliminary balance.

Describing client balances

If you entered client unpaid receipt aggregates when you set up the clients — which is the thing that I suggest — you've just described your client balances. You, old buddy, can jump to the following segment, "Describing seller balances."

If you didn't enter client unpaid receipt aggregates, you have to supply that data before you conclude the Chart of Account data. To do this, open the receipt in the standard way, which I describe in Chapter 4. The one essential job is to use the first receipt date when you enter the receipt.

Describing merchant balances

If you entered seller unpaid bill sums when you set up the merchants — which is additionally what I suggest prior — you described your merchant balances. In which case, you can jump to the following segment, "Covering some accounting silliness."

Disguising some accounting ridiculousness

After you enter the client and merchant balances into QuickBooks, you have to enter the remainder of the preliminary balance, which you do by making two significant strides. In the initial step, you cover a few silly accounts, called tension accounts, which QuickBooks makes when you set up the Item, Customer, and Vendor accounts. The subsequent advance, which I describe in the accompanying segment, is providing the last scarcely any missing numbers.

You can deliver your half-complete preliminary balance from inside QuickBooks by tapping the Report Center symbol and picking Reports ⇒ Accountants and Taxes ⇒ Trial Balance. QuickBooks shows the preliminary balance report in a record window.

If you have to do such, enter the change date in the From box by tapping the container and writing the transformation date in MM/DD/YYYY position. You can set the From box to any esteem; the From and To extend simply needs to end with the transformation date. Make a note of the credit and charge balances that appeared for the Uncategorized Income and Uncategorized Expenses accounts.

If you need it, you can print the report by tapping the Print button; then, when QuickBooks shows the Print Report transaction box, click its Print button. Indeed, you click two Print buttons.

After you have the transformation date balances for the Uncategorized Income and Uncategorized

Expenses accounts, you're prepared to make the group's accounting modification. To do as such, follow these means:

1. From the home screen, either click the Chart of Accounts symbol in the Company territory or pick Lists ⇒ Chart of Accounts to show the Chart of Accounts window.

2. Double-tap Opening Balance Equity in the Chart of Accounts list to confirm that account.

Opening Balance Equity is recorded after the obligation accounts. QuickBooks shows the register — a list of transactions — for the Opening Balance Equity account.

3. Select the following empty column of the register if it isn't now chosen (even though it most likely is).

You can choose a line by clicking it, or you can use the up-or down-button key to move to the following empty column.

4. Type the transformation date in the Date field.

Move the cursor to the Date field (if it isn't as of now there), and type the date. Use MM/DD/YYYY position. You can type either 06302019 or 6/30/2019 to enter June 30, 2019.

5. Type the Uncategorized Income account balance (from the preliminary balance report) in the Increase field.

6. Type Uncategorized Income (the record name) in the Account field.

Select the Account field, which is on the column beneath the word Payee, and start writing Uncategorized Income, the record name. When you type enough of the name for QuickBooks to make sense of what you're writing, it fills in the remainder of the name for you. When this occurs, you can quit writing.

7. Click the Record button to record the Uncategorized Income modification transaction.

Once more, select the following empty line of the register.

8. Click the line or use the up-or down-button key.

9. Type the transformation date in the Date field.

Move the cursor to the Date field (if it isn't as of now there) and type the date. You use the MM/DD/YYYY group. You can type 6/30/2019, for instance, to enter June 30, 2019.

10. Type the Uncategorized Expenses account balance in the Decrease field.

11. Type Uncategorized Expenses (the record name) in the Account field.

Select the Account field, which is on the second line of the register transaction, and start writing Uncategorized Expenses, the record name. When you type enough of the name for QuickBooks to make sense of what you're writing, it fills in the remainder of the name for you.

12. Click the Record button to record the Uncategorized Expenses change transaction.

You can close the Opening Balance Equity register now. You're done with it. One approach to close it is to tap the Close button in the upper right corner of the window.

You can check your work up to this point — and checking it is a smart thought — by delivering another copy of the preliminary balance report. What you need to check is the Uncategorized Income, and Uncategorized Expenses account balances. The two of them ought to be zero.

If the Uncategorized Income and the Uncategorized Expenses account balances don't show zero, we might have bungled the collection modification. To fix the mix-up, redisplay the Opening Balance Equity register (as noted prior, you can double-tap Opening Balance Equity in the Chart of Accounts list to show that account). Select the modification transactions; and afterward check the record, sum, and field (Increase or Decrease). If one of the fields isn't right, select the field and replace its substance by writing over it.

One other point. QuickBooks may show different accounts in its preliminary balance (contingent upon how you set up the QuickBooks document). You don't have to stress over these different accounts, in any case. You just need to ensure that the Uncategorized Income and Uncategorized Expense account balance equals zero after your alterations.

Providing the missing numbers

You're nearly done. Truly. Your last errand is to enter the remainder of the preliminary balance sums into QuickBooks. To play out this assignment, you have to have an initial balance arranged as of the change date. If you adhered to my directions in Chapter 2, you have one. Follow this means:

1. Pick either Company ⇒ Makes General Journal Entries or Accountant ⇒ Make General Journal

Entries. QuickBooks shows the Make General Journal Entries window.

2. Type the transformation date in the Date field.

Move the cursor to the Date field (if it isn't now there), and type the date. As you would know, at this point, you use the MM/DD/YYYY design. You can type 6/30/2019 for June 30, 2019, for instance (or 06302019, if you would prefer not to place in the slices).

3. Type every preliminary balance record and balance that isn't as of now in the half-finished initial balance.

Alright. This progression sounds befuddling. In any case, recollect that you've just entered your money, accounts of sales, stock, and accounts payable record balances; maybe even a couple of other record balances; and a segment of the Opening Balance Equity account balance as a significant aspect of QuickBooks Setup.

Presently you have to enter the remainder of the preliminary balance — explicitly, the year-to-date pay and business ledger balances, any missing resources or liabilities, and the rest of the segment of the Opening Balance Equity. To enter each record and stability, use a column of the Make General Journal Entries window list box.

4. Click the Save and New button to record the general diary sections that set up the remainder of your preliminary balance.

Checking your work once again

Twofold checking your work is a smart thought. Produce another copy of the preliminary balance report, and watch that the QuickBooks initial balance is a similar one that you needed to enter.

You can deliver a preliminary balance by picking Reports ⇒ Accountant and Taxes ⇒ Trial Balance. Make sure to enter the transformation date in the as of content box. If the QuickBooks preliminary offset report concurs with what your accounts appear, you're done.

Congrats! You're finished.

Chapter Four: Fundamental Steps to Using Quickbook 2

Right now (may be shocked to find), I describe how to make and print invoices in QuickBooks, just as how to create and print credit updates.

You use the QuickBooks receipt form to charge clients for the merchandise and ventures that you sell. You use its credit updates form to deal with returns and dropped orders for which you've gotten installments.

Ensuring That You're Ready to Invoice Customers

I realize that you're most likely set to go. On the whole, you have to check a couple of things, alright? Great.

You ought to have introduced QuickBooks. You ought to have set up an organization and a Chart of Accounts in QuickBooks Setup, as I describe in Chapter 2. You additionally ought to have entered every one of your lists and your beginning preliminary parity or convinced your bookkeeper to register it for you, as I describe in Chapter 3.

For whatever length of time that you've done so much essential stuff, you're prepared to begin. If you don't have one of the requirements done, you have to finish it before going any further.

Sorry. I don't make the principles. I simply mention to you what they are.

Setting up an Invoice

After you complete all the major work, setting up a receipt with QuickBooks is a simple task. If clicking buttons and filling in content boxes are turning out to be routine to you, avoid the accompanying in-depth editorial and just showcase the Create Invoices window — either by picking Customers

⇒ Create Invoices or tapping the Invoices symbol on the home page. When filling right now, clicks the Print button. If you need more assistance than a solitary sentence gives, continue reading for a bit by bit guidelines.

In the accompanying steps, I describe how to make the most confounded and included receipt around: an item receipt. A few fields in the item receipt don't show up in the administration or expert receipt; however, don't stress over whether your business is administration or expert.

Making a help or expert receipt works a similar way fundamentally as making an item receipt; you simply fill in fewer fields. Furthermore, remember that you start with Steps 1 and 2 regardless of what kind of receipt you make. Right away, here's the way to make a receipt:

1. Show the Create Invoices window by picking Customers ⇒ Create Invoices.

2. Select the format or receipt form that you need to use from the Template drop-down list.

QuickBooks accompanies predefined receipt form types, including Product, Professional, Service, and (contingent upon how you set up QuickBooks and which variant of QuickBooks you're using) a bunch of other particular receipt formats. Which one shows up, of course, relies upon what you informed QuickBooks regarding your business during QuickBooks Setup. You can likewise make your custom receipt layout (or change a current one). I describe editing receipt forms in the "Redoing Your Invoices and Credit Memos" segment later right now.

3. Distinguish the client and, if necessary, the job by using the Customer:Job drop-down list.

Look through the Customer:Job drop-down list until you see the client or occupation name that you need; when click it.

4. (Discretionary) Assign a class to the receipt.

If you use classes to follow costs and salary, activate the Class drop-down list and select a suitable class for the receipt. To turn this helpful method for sorting transactions on or off (which is needless excess for specific organizations), pick Edit ⇒ Preferences, click Accounting on the left, click the Company Preferences tab, and afterward select or clear the Use Class Tracking checkbox.

5. Give the receipt date.

Press Tab a few times to move the cursor to the Date content box. When entering the right date in MM/DD/YYYY position. You likewise can use the accompanying mystery codes to change the date:

Press + (the in addition to the image) to push the date forward one day.

Press – (the short image) to move the go back one day.

Press T to change the date to the present date (as indicated by the framework time that your PC's internal clock gives).

Press M to change the date to the first day of the month (because M is the central letter in the word month).

Press H to change the date to the most recent day of the month (since H is the last letter in the word month).

Press Y to change the date to the first day of the year (because, as you no uncertainty can figure, Y is the central letter in the word year).

Press R to change the date to the most recent day of the year (since R is the last letter in the word year).

You can likewise tap the button at the correct finish of the Date field to show a truncated schedule. To choose a date from the schedule, simply click the date you need. Click the buttons in the upper left and upper right corners of the schedule to show the past or one month from now.

6. (Discretionary) Enter a receipt number in the Invoice # content box.

QuickBooks recommends a receipt number by adding 1 to the last receipt number that you used. You can acknowledge this expansion or, if you have to have it your way, tab to the Invoice # content box and change the number to anything you desire.

7. Fix the Bill To address, if necessary.

QuickBooks snatches the charging address from the Customer list. You can change the location for the receipt by supplanting some part of the standard charging address. You can, for instance, embed a different line that says Attention: William Bobbins, if that is the name of the individual to whom the receipt ought to go.

8. Fix the Ship-To address, if essential.

I feel like a messed up record, yet here's the alignment: QuickBooks likewise snatches the transportation address from the Customer list. So if the transportation address has something abnormal about it for only this one receipt, you can change the location by supplanting or adding data to the Ship-To address square. Note that QuickBooks will monitor every one of the transportation tends to you use for a client, so if you used a delivery address previously, you might have the option to choose it from the Ship-To drop-down list.

9. (Discretionary kind of) Provide the buy request number in the P.O. Number content box.

If the client issues buy orders (POs), enter the quantity of the buy request that approves this buy. (Only for the record, PO is articulated pee-goodness, not poh or crap.)

10. Determine the installment terms by choosing an alternative from the Terms drop-down list.

11. (Discretionary) Name the salesperson.

Rep doesn't represent notoriety, so don't put three-letter article remarks here (even though I'd love to perceive what you can do with three letters). If you need to follow sales by agent, use the Rep drop-down list. Mostly initiate the list by clicking its button and afterward pick a name. Salespeople can incorporate representatives, yet they can likewise incorporate others whom you've entered in your different records. To rapidly include an agent, select Add New and afterward use the helpful dandy transaction boxes that QuickBooks shows. To work with the Sales Rep list, pick Lists ⇒ Customer, and Vendor Profile Lists ⇒ Sales Rep List.

12. Indicate the delivery date if it's an option that is other than the receipt date.

To indicate the date, just move the cursor to the Ship content box and afterward type the date in MM/DD/YYYY group. You can move the cursor by squeezing Tab or by tapping the content box.

13. Indicate the delivery strategy.

You can most likely think about how you indicate the transportation strategy, however equal form and a recurring character drive me to proceed. So to determine the delivery technique, move the cursor to the via the drop-down list and afterward select a transportation strategy from it.

Coincidentally, you can add new transporting strategies to the list by choosing Add New and afterward rounding out the charming little discourse box that QuickBooks shows. Setting up the original transporting plan is extremely simple.

14. Determine the FOB point by using the F.O.B. content box.

Dandy represents free ready. The FOB point is a higher priority than it initially appears — in any event in marketing prudence — because the FOB point decides when the transaction of possession happens, who pays cargo, and who bears the dangers of harm to the merchandise during transportation.

If a shipment is free ready at the delivery point, the responsibility for products being offered moves to the buyer when the merchandise leaves the vender's transportation dock. (Recall that you're the merchant.) For this situation, the buyer pays the cargo and bears the danger of delivery harm. You can indicate the FOB shipping point either as FOB Shipping Point or by using the name of the city. If the transportation point is Seattle, for instance, FOB Seattle is a similar thing as FOB Shipping Point. Most products are dispatched as FOB Shipping Point, incidentally.

If a shipment is free ready at the goal point, the responsibility for products that are being offered moves to the buyer when the merchandise land on the buyer's transportation dock. The vender pays the cargo and bears the danger of delivery harm. You can determine the FOB goal point either as FOB Destination Point or by using the name of the city. If the goal point is Omaha, for instance, FOB Omaha is a similar thing as FOB Destination Point.

15. Enter everything that you're selling.

Move the cursor to the first line of the Quantity/Item Code/Description/Price Each/Amount/Tax list box. (OK, I realize that is not a generally great name for it, yet you comprehend what I mean, right?) You have to begin filling in the details that go into the receipt. After you move the cursor to a line in the list box, QuickBooks transforms the Item Code field into a drop-down list. Activate the Item Code drop-down list of the first empty column in the list box and afterward select the thing.

When you select the thing, QuickBooks fills in the Description and Price Each content boxes with whatever business description and sales cost you've entered in the Item list. (You can alter the data for this specific receipt if you have to.) Enter the number of things sold in the Quantity content box. (After you enter this number, QuickBooks ascertains the sum by duplicating Quantity by Price Each.) If you need different things in the receipt, use the staying void columns of the list box to enter everyone. If you chose the Taxable checkbox when you added the thing to the Item list, the word Tax shows up in the Tax segment to demonstrate that the thing will be saddled. If the thing is nontaxable (or you want to be an assessment dodger out of the blue), click the Tax section, and choose None.

You can put the same number of things in a receipt as you need. If you need more space on a single page, QuickBooks includes the same amount of pages as necessary to the receipt. Data about the receipt aggregate goes just on the last page.

16. Enter any unusual things that the receipt ought to incorporate.

If you haven't worked much with the QuickBooks thing record, you have no clue what I'm discussing. (For more data about adding to and working with files in QuickBooks, go through Chapter 3.)

To describe any of the unusual things, activate the Item Code drop-down list of the following void line and afterward select the extraordinary thing. After QuickBooks fills in the Description and Price Each content boxes, alter this data (if essential). Describe every one of the other exceptional things — subtotals, limits, cargo, etc. — that you're organizing in the receipt by filling in the empty lines in the list box.

17. (Discretionary) Add a client message.

Click the Customer Message box, activate its drop-down list, and select a quick client message. To add client messages to the Customer Message list, select the Add New alternative and afterward fill in the discourse box that QuickBooks shows. Click OK when you're set. (I realize that I talk about the Customer Message confine Chapter 3, yet I needed to rapidly describe how to include a client message again with the goal that you don't need to flip back through a lot of pages.)

18. Determine the business charge.

If you determined an assessment rate in the Customer list, QuickBooks uses it as a default. If it isn't right, move the cursor to the Tax list box, initiate the drop-down menu, and select the correct sales charge.

19. (Really discretionary) Add an update.

You can add a reminder description to the receipt if you need to. This update doesn't print in invoices — just in the Customer Statement. Update descriptions give you a method for putting away data identified with a receipt with that receipt.

20. If you need to defer printing this receipt, select the Print Later checkbox that shows up on the lace of buttons and boxes over the principle part of the Create Invoices window.

I need to defer discussing what choosing the Print Later checkbox does until I finish the discussion of receipt creation. I talk about printing invoices somewhat later in the section. I guarantee.

21. Save the receipt by tapping the Save and New button or the Save and Close button at the base of the window.

QuickBooks saves the receipt that is onscreen. If you click Save and New, QuickBooks shows a void Create Invoices window with the goal that you can make another receipt.

You can page to and fro through invoices that you made before by tapping the Next and Previous buttons (which resemble left and right buttons).

When you're finished making invoices, you can tap the receipt form's Save and Close button or press the Escape key.

Fixing Invoice Mistakes

I'm not a perfect individual. You're — well, you know this, right? — Not a perfect individual. Hell, no one is; everybody commits errors. You don't have to get worked up over mix-ups that you make while entering data in invoices, however, because in the accompanying segments, I tell you the best way to fix the most widely recognized slip-ups that you may make in your invoices.

If the receipt is still shown onscreen

If the receipt is still shown on screen, you can simply move the cursor to the container or button that is off-base and afterward fix the misstep. Since a large portion of the bits of data that you enter in the Create Invoices window are quick and painless, you can undoubtedly supplant the substance of specific fields by composing over anything that's as of now there. To start from the very beginning once more, simply click the Clear button at the base of the screen. To save the receipt after you've rolled out your improvements, click the Save and New button.

If the receipt isn't shown onscreen

If the receipt isn't shown onscreen, and you haven't yet printed it, you can use the Next and Previous buttons (which show up on the Main tab and show pictures of left-pointing and right-pointing buttons) to page through the invoices. When you find a good pace with the blunder, basically fix the mistake as I describe in the previous segment. If you make a mistake setting the receipt, you can tap the Revert button to return to the saved receipt. The Revert button replaces the Clear button when you see a current receipt — that is, a receipt that you've just saved.

If you printed the receipt, you additionally could cause the kind of progress that I to describe in the above passages. You can page through the invoices until you locate the one (presently printed) that has the blunder, for instance, and afterward right the mistake and print the receipt once more. I'm not entirely sure that you need to go this course if you've just sent the receipt, in any case. You might need to think about fixing the receipt by giving either a credit notice (if the first receipt cheated) or another receipt (if the first receipt undercharged). The motivation behind why I propose giving a credit update or another receipt is that life gets untidy if you and your client have various copies of a similar receipt skimming around and causing disarray. (I tell you the best way to give a credit notice in the fittingly titled area "Setting up a Credit Memo" later right now.)

Erasing a receipt

I delay to refer to this; however, you likewise can erase invoices. Procedurally, erasing a receipt is straightforward. You simply show the receipt in the Create Invoices window and afterward click the Delete window or pick Edit ⇒ Delete Invoice.

When QuickBooks requests that you affirm your erasure, click Yes. Read the following section first, however, because you might not have any desire to erase the receipt.

Even though erasing invoices is simple, it isn't something that you ought to do calmly or for no particular reason. Deleting a receipt is alright if you've quite recently made it, just you have seen it, and you haven't yet printed it. Right now, one has to realize that you've committed an error. It's your mystery. The remainder of the time — regardless of whether you make a receipt that you don't need later — you should keep a copy of the receipt in the QuickBooks framework. Doing so gives a record that the receipt existed, which for the most part, makes it simpler to address addresses later.

"However, how would I write my books if I leave the sham receipt?" you inquire.

Great inquiry. To address your budgetary records for the receipt that you would prefer not to check any longer, necessarily void the receipt. The receipt stays in the QuickBooks framework, yet QuickBooks doesn't tally it because the receipt loses its amount and sum data. Uplifting news — voiding a receipt is as necessary as erasing one. Simply show the receipt in the Create Invoices window and afterward pick Edit ⇒ Void Invoice. Or on the other hand, click the drop-down button beneath the Delete window and select Void from the menu that QuickBooks shows.

Setting up a Credit Memo

Credit updates can be helpful ways to fix information passage messes up that you didn't discover or address prior. Credit notices are likewise convenient ways to deal with things like client returns and discounts. If you've arranged a receipt or two in your time, you'll see that setting up a QuickBooks credit update is significantly simpler than using antiquated strategies.

In the accompanying steps, I describe how to make the most confused and included sort of credit notice: an item credit update. Making a help or expert credit reminder works a similar way, primarily, in any case. You simply fill in fewer fields.

To make an item credit notice, follow these means:

1. Pick Customers ⇒ Create Credit Memos/Refunds or click the Refunds and Credits symbol in the Customer segment of the landing page to show the Create Credit Memos/Refunds window

2. Distinguish the client and, if vital, the job in the Customer:Job drop-down list.

You can choose the client or employment from the list by clicking it.

3. (Discretionary) Specify a class for the credit reminder.

In case you're using classes to arrange transactions, activate the Class drop-down list and pick the fitting class for the credit update.

4. Date the credit reminder (albeit going consistent is discretionary).

Press Tab to move the cursor to the Date content box. Then enter the right date in MM/DD/YYYY design. You likewise can use the mystery date-altering codes that I describe in the area "Setting up an Invoice" before the section.

5. (Discretionary) Enter a credit notice number.

QuickBooks recommends a credit update number by adding 1 to the last credit reminder number you used. You can acknowledge the number or tab to the Credit No. content box to change the number to anything you desire.

6. Fix the Customer address, if fundamental.

QuickBooks gets the charging address from the Customer list. You can change the location for the credit notice by supplanting some part of the typical charging address. Usually, you should use a similar location for the credit notice that you handle for the first receipt or invoices.

7. (Discretionary kind of) Provide the PO number.

If the credit update alters the all-out residual parity on a client PO, you ought to presumably enter the quantity of the PO into the P.O. No. content box.

8. If the client returns things, describe everything.

Move the cursor to the central column of the Item/Description/Qty/Rate/Amount/Tax content box. In the first void column of the case, enact the Item drop-down list and afterward select the thing. After you choose it, QuickBooks fills in the Description and Rate content boxes with whatever business description and sales value you entered in the Item list. (You can alter this data if you need; however, it isn't vital.) Enter the number of things that the client is returning (or not paying for) in the Qty content box. (After you enter this number, QuickBooks ascertains the sum by increasing Qty by Rate.) Enter everything that the client is returning by filling in the empty lines of the list box.

Similarly, as with invoices, you can put the same number of things in an acknowledged reminder as you need. If you need more space on a single page, QuickBooks continues adding pages to the credit update until you're done. The all-out data goes on the last page.

9. Describe any unique things that the credit notice ought to incorporate.

If you need to give a credit notice for different things that show up in the first receipt — cargo, limits, various charges, etc. — add descriptions of everything to the Item list.

To include descriptions of these things, initiate the Item drop-down list of the following void column and afterward select the rare occurrence. (You actuate the menu by tapping the field once to transform it into a drop-down list and later tapping the fields down button to get to the list.) After QuickBooks fills in the Description and Rate content boxes, alter this data (if essential).

Enter every unusual thing — subtotal, markdown, cargo, etc. — that you're organizing in the credit notice.

If you need to incorporate a Discount thing, you have to put a Subtotal thing in the credit update after the stock or different things that you've limited. Then stick a Discount thing straightforwardly after the Subtotal thing.

When you do this, QuickBooks computes the markdown as a level of the subtotal.

10. (Discretionary) Add a client message.

Initiate the Customer Message list and select a smart client message.

11. Indicate the business charge.

Move the cursor to the Tax list box, actuate the list box, and afterward, select the right sales charge.

12. (Discretionary, however, a great thought) Add an update.

You can use the Memo content box to add an update description to the credit notice. You may use this description to clarify your purposes behind giving the credit update and to cross-reference the first receipt or invoices, for instance. Note that the Memo field prints in the Customer Statement.

13. If you need to defer printing this credit notice, select the Print Later checkbox.

I need to defer discussing what choosing the Print Later checkbox does until I finish the discussion of credit reminder creation. The inclusion of printing invoices and credit reminders comes up in a later segment.

14. Save the credit update.

To save a finished credit update, click either the Save and New or Save and Close button. QuickBooks then shows a transaction box that asks what you need to do with the credit reminder:

Retain the credit, give a discount, or apply the credit to a receipt. Settle on your decision by tapping the button that compares to what you need to do. If you pick Apply to Invoice, QuickBooks requests some extra data. QuickBooks then saves the onscreen credit update and, if you clicked Save and New, shows a void Create Credit Memos/Refunds window with the goal that you can make another credit reminder. (Note that you can page to and fro through credit notices that you created before by tapping the Next and Previous buttons.) When you're finished making credit notices, you can tap the credit update form's Close button.

Fixing Credit Memo Mistakes

Indeed, I can rehash a similar data that I give you in "Fixing Invoice Mistakes," prior right now, leave you with a peculiar sentiment of history repeating itself. However, I won't.

History Lessons

In the first place, QuickBooks allows you to include and evacuate this verifiable data about a client from the Create Invoices window, the Create

123

Credit Memos/Refunds window, and most other client data windows. To, on the other hand, include and afterward evacuate verifiable data about a client to a window, click the sharpened stone button that shows up in the upper left corner of the board beside the client's name.

A subsequent clicky point: If you have a moment or two after you've used QuickBooks a piece, feel free to tap the buttons that show up inside the chronicled data board. These buttons permit you to penetrate down and get more data about a recorded transaction, for instance.

Printing Invoices and Credit Memos

As a significant aspect of setting up QuickBooks, you chose a receipt type. I accept that you have the crude paper stock for whatever receipt type you picked. In case you're going to print on clear letterhead, for instance, I expect that you have a letterhead lying around. If you choose to use preprinted forms, I accept that you've requested those forms and have gotten them.

I additionally accept that you've just set up your printer. If you've at any point printed anything, your printer is now set up. Truly.

Stacking the forms into the printer

This part is simple. Just burden the receipt forms into the printer a similar way you generally load paper. Since you have one of about a jillion various printers, I can't give you the exact advances that you have to follow; however, if you've used a printer a piece, you ought to have no issue.

Setting up the receipt printer

You have to set up the receipt printer just once; however, you have to indicate a bunch of general receipts printing rules. These standards likewise apply to credit notices and buy orders, coincidentally.

To set up your printer for receipt printing, follow these means:

1. Pick File ⇒ Printer Setup.

2. From the Form Name drop-down list, select Invoice.

3. Select the printer that you need to use to print invoices.

Actuate the Printer Name drop-down list to see the introduced printers. Select the one that you need to use for printing invoices and buy orders.

4. (Discretionary) Select the printer type.

The Printer Type drop-down list describes the sort of paper that your printer employments. You have two options:

Constant: Your paper comes as one associated ream with damaged edges.

Page-Oriented: Your paper is on single sheets.

5. Select the sort of receipt form.

Select the alternative button that describes the sort of form that you need to print on: Intuit Preprinted Forms, Blank Paper, or Letterhead. Then select the Do Not Print Lines around Each Field checkbox if you don't care for the decent boxes that QuickBooks makes to isolate each field.

6. (Discretionary, however, a great thought) Print a test receipt on genuine receipt paper.

Click the Align button. When QuickBooks shows the Align Printer discourse box, pick the sort of receipt that you need to print and afterward click OK. When QuickBooks shows the Fine Alignment transaction box, click the Print Sample button to advise QuickBooks to print a spurious receipt on whatever paper you've stacked in the receipt printer.

The spurious receipt that QuickBooks prints allow you to perceive what your invoices will resemble. The receipt additionally has a lot of alignment gridlines that prints over the Bill To content box. You can use these gridlines if you have to fine-adjust your printer.

7. Fix any form of alignment issues.

If you see any alignment issues after you complete step 6, you have to fix them. (Alignment issues usually happen just with sway printers.

With laser printers or inkjet printers, pieces of paper feed into the printer a similar way without fail, so you never need to mess with the form alignment.)

To fix any huge alignment issues — like stuff imprinting in an inappropriate spot — you have to modify how the paper sustains into the printer. When you at long last get the paper stacked decently well, make sure to note precisely how you have it stacked. You have to have the printer and paper set up a similar way every time you print.

For minor (however, in any case irritating) alignment issues, use the Fine Alignment discourse box's Vertical and Horizontal boxes to modify the form's alignment. Then print another example receipt. Feel free to test a piece. You have to tweak the printing of the receipt form just once.

Click OK in the Fine Alignment discourse box when you finish coming back to the Printer Setup transaction box.

Tapping the Options button in the Printer Setup discourse box opens the chose printer's Windows printer alignment data, where you can do such things as determine quality settings or print request. Since this data identifies with Windows and not to QuickBooks, I'm not going to clarify it. If you're the curious kind, or if you inadvertently click it and then have inquiries concerning what you see, allude either to your Windows client's guide or the printer's client's guide.

8. Save your printer settings stuff.

After you complete the process of tinkering with all the Printer Setup discourse box settings, click OK to save your changes.

If you generally need to use some specific settings to print a particular form (perhaps you usually print two duplicates of a receipt, for instance), see the "Redoing Your Invoices and Credit Memos" segment later right now.

You can print invoices and credit notices, each in turn or a bunch. How you print them has no effect on QuickBooks or to me, your unassuming writer. Pick the route that appears to accommodate your style best. The accompanying segments give you how.

Printing invoices and acknowledge notices as you make them

If you need to print invoices and accept reminders as you make them, follow these means:

1. Click the Print button after you make the receipt or credit notice.

After you fill in the containers of the Create Invoices window or the Create Credit Memos/Refunds window, click the Print button. QuickBooks, ever the dependable hireling, shows either the Print One Invoice discourse box or the Print One Credit Memo/Refund transaction box, which looks practically like the Print One Invoice discourse box.

2. (Discretionary) Select the sort of receipt or credit update form.

In case you're utilizing an alternate sort of receipt or credit update form than you've described for the receipt printer alignment, select the kind of form that you need to print from the Print On choice button decisions. You can choose Intuit Preprinted Forms, Blank Paper, or Letterhead.

You shouldn't need to stress over printing test receipt or credit notice frames or tinkering with form alignment issues if you tend to these issues when you set up the receipt printer, so I'm not going to discuss the Align button here. If you need to do this sort of stuff and you need assistance, allude to the former segment, "Setting up the receipt printer," in which I describe how to print test forms and fix form alignment issues.

3. Print the form.

Click the Print button to send the form to the printer.

4. Audit the receipt or credit reminder, and republish the form if fundamental.

Audit the receipt or credit reminder to see whether QuickBooks printed it accurately. If the form looks wrong, fix whatever caused the issue (maybe you printed it on an inappropriate paper, for instance) and reproduce the form by tapping the Print button once more.

Printing invoices in a cluster

If you need to print invoices in a group, you have to check the Print Later check the box that shows up on the Create Invoices window's lace. This check mark advises QuickBooks to place a duplicate of the receipt in an extraordinary invoices to-be-printed list.

When you later need to print the invoices to-be-printed list, follow these means:

1. Show the Create Invoices window (pick Customers ⇒ Create Invoices), click the button by the Print button, and pick Batch starting from the drop list.

QuickBooks shows the Select Invoices to Print discourse box. This container records all the invoices that you've set apart as Print Later and hasn't yet printed.

2. Select the invoices that you need to print.

At first, QuickBooks denotes all the invoices with a checkmark, showing that they'll be printed. You can choose and deselect single invoices on the list by clicking them. You likewise can tap the Select All button (to check all the invoices) or the Select None button (to deselect all the invoices).

3. Click OK.

After you effectively mark all the invoices you need to print — and none of the ones you would prefer not to print — click OK. QuickBooks shows the Print Invoices transaction box.

4. (Discretionary) Select the sort of receipt form.

If you use an alternate sort of receipt form from the variety, you depicted during receipt alignment, select the kind of form that you need to print on by utilizing the Print On alternatives. You can pick Intuit Preprinted Forms, Blank Paper, or Letterhead.

For additional on these sorts of forms, read the sidebar "What am I imprinting on?" prior right now.

5. Print the forms.

Click the Print button to send the chose receipt forms to the printer. QuickBooks prints the forms and afterward shows a message box that asks whether the forms printed expertly.

6. Survey the receipt forms, and reproduce them if fundamental.

Audit the invoices to see whether QuickBooks printed them all accurately. If all the forms look alright, click OK in the message box. If at least one forms don't look OK, enter the receipt number of the main off base form in the message box. Then fix whatever issue messed up the form (maybe you printed it on an inappropriate paper, for instance) and republish the awful form(s) by tapping the Print button once more. (The Print button is in the Print Invoices discourse box.)

Printing credit reminders in a clump

If you need to print credit updates in a clump, you have to choose the Print Later check the box that shows up on the Main tab of the Create Credit Memos/Refunds window. Selecting this checkbox advises QuickBooks to put a duplicate of the credit reminder on an exceptional credit notices to-be-printed list.

Printing credit notices in a group work comparably to printing invoices in a bunch. Since I describe how to print invoices in a bunch in the first area, right now, speed through a depiction of printing credit updates in a cluster. If you get lost or have questions, alluding to the first area.

When you're prepared to print the credit updates that are in the to-be-printed list, follow these means:

133

1. Show the Create Credit Memos/Refunds window, click the down button beside the Print button, and select Batch starting from the drop list. QuickBooks shows the Select Credit Memos to Print transaction box.

2. Select the credit reminders that you need to print.

3. Click OK to display the Print Credit Memos discourse box.

4. Use the Print Credit Memos discourse box to describe how you need your credit notices to be printed.

5. Click the Print button to send the chose credit reminders to the printer. QuickBooks prints the credit notices.

Sending Invoices and Credit Memos using Email

If you have an email previously set up on your PC, you can email invoices as opposed to print them directly from inside QuickBooks. Right now, email a receipt or credit notice, click the Email button, which shows up on the Main tab of the Create Invoices window.

To send your receipt through email, enter the email address of the business that you need to bill or discount cash to, alter the message as suitable (make a point to click that Check Spelling button), and afterward click the Send button.

You can likewise fax invoices and credit updates from inside QuickBooks if you have fax-transmission programming introduced. To do this, click the Print button at the highest point of the Create Invoices or Create Credit Memos/Refunds window, pick your fax programming from the Printer Name drop-down list, and afterward use the wizard that seems to send the fax using your modem. (Transmission charges may apply.)

Modifying Your Invoices and Credit Memos

With QuickBooks, you can without much of a stretch redo the receipt and credit reminder layouts, or you can make new invoices and credit notices dependent on one of the current QuickBooks formats. You should simply open the form that you need to tweak, click the Formatting tab, and afterward click the Customize Design button. QuickBooks shows an Intuit page that strolls you through the means for making your own exceptionally tweaked form.

On the other hand, you can tap the Formatting tab and afterward click its Customize Data Layout button. When QuickBooks asks whether you're alright with working with a duplicate of the default form format, click the Make Copy button. QuickBooks shows the Additional Customization discourse box, which gives a lot of checkboxes and message boxes you can use to redo away. The Additional Customization discourse box likewise provides a preview with the territory that shows what your customizations resemble, so freak out, and be bold. (If you make a wreck, simply click Cancel to relinquish your altered changes. Then, if you need, restart the procedure — may be somewhat shrewder and more intelligent for the experience.)

Chapter Six: Printing Checks

Printing checks in QuickBooks is brisk. Indeed, it's brisk after you set up your printer accurately. If you have a constant feed printer, you know at this point these printers have issues printing anything on a form. The alignment consistently gets failed.

QuickBooks has check forms that you can purchase, and I suggest utilizing them if you print checks. The QuickBooks checks were made to work with this program. And all banks acknowledge these checks.

Preparing the Printer

Before you can begin printing checks, you need to ensure that your printer is set up to print them. You likewise need to disclose to QuickBooks what to put on the checks: your organization name, address, logo, etc. Furthermore, you may have a go at running a couple of test checks through the wringer to see whether they turn out good.

Follow these means to set up the printer:

1. Pick File ⇒ Printer Setup.

After you pick this direction, you see the Printer Setup transaction box.

2. Select Check/PayCheck from the Form Name drop-down list.

QuickBooks sets your printing choices diversely, relying upon which form you need to print. For printing checks, you need to choose the Check/PayCheck form from the Form Name drop-down list at the highest point of the discourse box.

3. From the Printer Name drop-down list, select your printer.

From the Printer Name drop-down list, click the down button and look at the printer names. When you introduced QuickBooks, it had an everyday programming to-programming chat with Windows to discover what sort of printer(s) you have, in addition to other things. Your printer is most likely previously chosen; if it isn't, select the right printer.

4. Set the right Printer Type alternative, if necessary.

This container is most likely previously filled in, as well, on account of that candid conversation that I notice in Step 3. In any case, if it isn't, click the down button and afterward pick Continuous or Page-Oriented. (The previous is by and large for spot framework printers, and the last is for laser and inkjet printers, however, it exceptionally just relies upon what sort of paper you use for your printer.)

5. Select the suitable Check Style.

Presently you're cooking. This progression is the place you find a workable pace good decision:

Voucher checks are a similar width as standard checks, yet there any longer. When you select the Voucher alternative, QuickBooks prints voucher data also: the things and costs organizations from the base of the Write Checks window.

QuickBooks likewise gives data about the financial records that you're composing this mind.

Standard checks are measured to fit in legitimate envelopes.

The Wallet alternative is for printing watches that are sufficiently little to fit in — you got it — a wallet.

6. (Discretionary) Click the Options button; modify your printer alternatives, and when you're done, click OK to come back to the Printer Setup discourse box.

After you click the Options button, QuickBooks shows your printer's Properties discourse box.

7. In the Properties discourse box, indicate print quality, number of duplicates, and different alternatives explicit to your printer. Then click OK to come back to the Printer Setup transaction box.

8. Click the Fonts tab of the Printer Setup discourse box and afterward the Fonts button on that tab to alter the textual styles on your checks.

When you click either the Font button or the Address Font button on this tab, you see the Select Font transaction box or the Select Address Font discourse box. You use the Address Font button to assign how your organization's name and address look and the Font button to assign what all other print on your checks resembles. Here's your opportunity to tidy up your checks and make your organization's name stick out.

Examination for some time with the Font, Font Style, and Size settings. If you have a book shop, for instance, pick the Bookman text style (possibly utilizing secure for your organization's name and address). If you run a flag-bearer administration, choose Courier; Italian mathematicians can use Times New Roman (only joking). You can perceive what your decisions resemble in the Sample box.

9. When you complete the process of messing around with the textual styles, click OK to return to the Printer Setup transaction box.

10. Click the Partial Page tab of the Printer Setup discourse box, and afterward select a Partial Page Printing Style.

Luckily, a few illustrations show up; else, you wouldn't understand what these alternatives are, OK? These choices are for the naturally cordial among you. Assume that you feed two checks to the printer; however, the check sheets have three checks each. You have a remaining check.

On account of this alternative, you can use the additional check. Select one of the options to reveal to QuickBooks how you intend to nourish the check to the printer — vertically on the left (the Side choice), vertically in the center (the Centered alternative), or on a flat plane (the Portrait choice). You feed checks to the printer in a similar way that you feed envelopes to it.

11. (Discretionary) Click the Logo window and afterward enter an organization logo or some clasp craft.

In the Logo transaction box, click File and afterward discover the index and BMP (bitmap) realistic record that you need to stack. Click OK. Note: Only illustrations that are in BMP alignment can be used on your checks, and Intuit prescribes that the logo be square.

12. (Discretionary) Click the Signature window and afterward enter a check signature picture.

Need to get incredibly courageous? Click the Signature button that shows up in the Printer Setup discourse box. When QuickBooks shows the Signature transaction box, click File and afterward discover the catalog and BMP (bitmap) realistic document with the mark that you need to stack. Click OK. Note: As with a logo, you can use a trademark here just if it's a BMP realistic.

13. Click OK when you're done.

That alignment was no Sunday excursion, right? In any case, your checks are on the whole fit to be printed, and you'll most likely never need to experience this difficulty again.

Printing a Check

For reasons unknown, when I find a good pace of the conversation, my heartbeat animates. Composing a check for genuine cash appears to be authentic. I get a similar inclination at whatever point I mail somebody money, regardless of whether the sum is ostensible.

I believe that the ideal approach to bring down my pulse (and yours, in case you're similar to me) is to print the darn check and be finished with it simply. QuickBooks can print checks in two different ways: as you think of them or in bundles.

First of all, in any case. Before you can print checks, you need to stack some unlimited free passes into your printer. This procedure works a similar path as stacking any paper into your printer. If you have questions, allude to your printer's documentation. (Sorry I can't help more on this procedure; however, a million distinct printers exist, and I can't tell which one you have, in any event, when I investigate my precious stone ball.)

A couple of words about printing checks

Check printing is somewhat confounded, right? For the record, I'm with you on this one. I genuinely wish it weren't such a lot of work, yet you'll see that printing checks get simpler after the first, not many occasions.

Indeed soon, you'll be running as opposed to strolling through the means. Entirely more quickly, you'll simply skate around such barriers as registration alignment.

Indeed soon, you'll know so much stuff and never need to read indeed more quickly again.

Printing a check as you write it

In case you're in the Write Checks window, and you've quite recently got done with rounding out a check, you can print it. The main disadvantage is that you need to print checks each in turn with this strategy. Here's the ticket:

1. Fill out your check.

Indeed, I firmly prescribe rounding out the check before printing it. Also, ensure that the Print Later checkbox is chosen.

2. Click the Print button in the Write Checks window. You see the Print Check discourse box.

3. Enter a check number in the Printed Check Number content box and afterward click OK.

After you click OK, you see the also named Print Checks discourse box. The settings that you find right now are the ones that you picked when you previously revealed to QuickBooks how to print checks. If you change the settings in the Print Checks transaction box, the progressions influence just this specific check. Whenever you print a check, you'll see your unique settings once more.

4. Click Print to acknowledge the default settings, or make changes in the discourse box and afterward click Print.

In the Printer Name field, indicate which printer you need to print to. In the Check Style territory, show whether you need to print a Voucher, Standard, or Wallet check.

In case you're printing an incomplete page of forms on a laser printer, use the Partial Page tab to show both the number of check forms on the fractional page and how you'll bolster them through your printer.

If you need your organization's name and address to show up on the check, select the Print Company Name and Address checkbox on the Settings tab.

After you click Print, QuickBooks prints the check, and you see the Print Checks — Confirmation transaction box. There's nothing precarious here — just a list of the watches that you simply attempted to print.

5. If the check didn't print accurately, follow these means:

a. Click the check recorded in the Print Checks — Confirmation discourse box to choose it and afterward click OK to come back to the Write Checks window.

b. Click the Write Checks window's Print button once more.

c. Enter the new check number and click Print once more.

Conclusion

This book is pressed with data about utilizing and profiting by QuickBooks.

Running or working in a private company is perhaps the most refreshing thing an individual can do. Truly. I would not joke about this. Of course, in some cases, nature is risky — sort of like the Old West — yet it's a situation wherein you have the chance to make vast amounts of cash. And, it's additionally a situation where you can construct an organization or a vocation that superbly fits you.

By examination, numerous siblings and sisters working in large organizations corporate America are aggressively attempting to accommodate their round pegs into agonizingly square gaps. Yuck.

This book isn't intended to be read from cover to cover like some James Patterson page-turner. Instead, it's sorted out into minor, no-sweat depictions of how you do the things you have to do. In case you're the kind of individual who simply doesn't feel right not perusing a book from cover to cover, you can (obviously) feel free to read this thing from front to back.

However, you likewise can use this book how you'd use a reference book. If you need to think about a subject, you can find it in the list of chapters; then, you can flip to the right section or page and read as much as you require or enjoy — no muss, straightforward.

I should specify a specific something; however: Accounting programming programs expect you to do a particular measure of readiness before you can use them to complete genuine work. If you haven't begun to use QuickBooks yet, I prescribe that you read the first parts of this book to discover what you have to do first.